Moore about Revelation

by
Charles R. Moore

DORRANCE PUBLISHING CO., INC
PITTSBURGH, PENNSYLVANIA 15222

ISBN # 0-8059-4205-X
Printed in the United States of America

First Printing

For information or to order additional books, please write:
Dorrance Publishing Co., Inc.
643 Smithfield Street
Pittsburgh, Pennsylvania 15222
U.S.A.

This book is dedicated to my wife, Judy Ann Moore, and my son, Robert Farley Moore.

MOORE ABOUT REVELATION

REVELATION- OUTLINE

CHAPTER 1

VS 1   REASON FOR WRITING THE BOOK

VS 2   WHO REVEALED THE THINGS TO COME TO PASS

VS 3   THE BLESSING OF THE ONES WHO READ THIS BOOK

VS 4-8 GREETING FROM JOHN THE WRITER

VS 9-18 THE POST-INCARNATE CHRIST IN HIS GLORIFIED BODY NO LONGER AS THE
        SAVIOR OF THE WORLD BUT AS THE JUDGE OF THIS WORLD.

VS 19   JOHN WILL SEE THE THINGS TO COME AND IS COMMANDED TO WRITE THEM
        DOWN.

VS 20   JESUS EXPLAINS WHAT JOHN HAS SEEN.

CHAPTER 2

VS 1-7 LETTER TO THE CHURCH AT EPHESUS.

VS 8-11 LETTER TO THE CHURCH AT SMYRNA.

VS 12-17 LETTER TO THE CHURCH AT PERGAMOS.

VS 18-29 LETTER TO THE CHURCH AT THYATIRA.

CHAPTER 3

VS 1-6 LETTER TO THE CHURCH AT SARDIS.

VS 7-13 LETTER TO THE CHURCH AT PHILADELPHIA.

VS 14-22 LETTER TO THE CHURCH AT LAODICEA.

CHAPTER 4

VS 1   THE SCENE CHANGES FROM THE EARTH TO HEAVEN, THE RAPTURE HAS
        HAPPENED. CHAPTER 4 TO CHAPTER 22:5 DEALS WITH THE PROPHESY THAT IS
        YET TO COME "THINGS THAT SHALL BE HEREAFTER."

VS 2   "IMMEDIATELY" IN THE TWINKLING OF THE EYE WE WILL BE CHANGED AND
        CAUGHT UP IN THE AIR TO BE WITH THE LORD IN HEAVEN.

VS 3-7 JOHN DESCRIBES WHAT HE SEES IN HEAVEN AROUND THE THRONE OF CHRIST.

VS 8-11 JOHN DESCRIBES THE PRAISE OF SAINTS AROUND THE THRONE.

CHAPTER 5

VS 1-4 THE BOOK WITH SEVEN SEALS.

VS 5--10 CHRIST AS OUR HIGH PRIEST IN HEAVEN IS THE ONLY ONE WHO CAN OPEN THE
        BOOK WHICH THE ONE ON THE THRONE HOLDS IN HIS RIGHT HAND.

VS 11-12 THE ANGLES PRAISE HIM THAT IS ABLE TO TAKE THE BOOK.

VS 13-14 THE UNIVERSE PRAISES HIM THAT LIVETH FOREVER AND EVER.

CHAPTER 6

VS 1   THE LAMB OF GOD OPENS THE BOOK WHICH CONTAINS THE JUDGMENTS OF GOD ON THE WHOLE EARTH FOR REJECTING HIS ONLY BEGOTTEN SON.

VS 2   THE OPENING OF THE FIRST SEAL AND THE RIDER ON A WHITE HORSE.

VS 3-4   THE OPENING OF THE SECOND SEAL AND THE RIDER ON A RED HORSE.

VS 5-6   THE OPENING OF THE THIRD SEAL AND THE RIDER ON A BLACK HORSE.

VS 7-8   THE OPENING OF THE FOURTH SEAL AND THE RIDER ON A PALE HORSE.

VS 9-11 THE OPENING OF THE FIFTH SEAL AND THE SOULS OF THEM THAT HAVE BEEN KILLED FOR THEIR TESTIMONY AND TRUSTING IN JESUS CHRIST TILL THIS TIME DURING THE TRIBULATION.

VS 12-17 THE OPENING OF THE SIXTH SEAL WHICH BEGINS THE WRATH OF THE LORD JESUS CHRIST ON THE INHABITANTS OF THE EARTH, BEGINNING THE SECOND HALF OF THE TRIBULATION (THE LAST THREE AND A HALF YEARS).

CHAPTER 7

JOHN INSERTS AN INTERLUDE BETWEEN THE SIXTH AND SEVENTH SEALS.

VS 1-3   TIME STANDS STILL WHILE JESUS SEALS HIS REMNANT.

VS 4-8   THE REMNANT IS REVEALED AS 144,000 JEWS FROM THE 12 TRIBES.

VS 9-17 THE SCENE CHANGES BACK TO HEAVEN WHERE A GREAT MULTITUDE OF THE SAVED ONES DURING THE TRIBULATION PRAISE JESUS. VS. 14.

CHAPTER 8

VS 1   THE OPENING OF THE SEVENTH SEAL AND REVEALING OF THE JUDGMENT TO COME ON THE INHABITANTS ON THE EARTH. THE FIRST SET OF SEVEN JUDGMENTS WITH SEVEN ANGELS WHICH ARE GIVEN SEVEN TRUMPETS.

VS 2-6   THE ANGEL AT THE ALTAR WITH A CENSER OF INCENSE.

VS 7   THE FIRST TRUMPET IS BLOWN AND ONE THIRD OF ALL TREES AND GRASS IS BURNED ON THE EARTH.

VS 8-9   THE SECOND TRUMPET IS BLOWN AND ONE THIRD OF THE SEAS BECOME BLOOD.

VS 10-11 THE THIRD TRUMPET IS BLOWN AND ONE THIRD OF ALL FRESH WATER BECOMES BITTER.

VS 12-13 THE FOURTH TRUMPET IS BLOWN AND THE SUN, MOON AND STARS ARE SMITTEN AND DARKENED TO SHINE FOR ONLY A THIRD PART OF THE DAY. THIS IS THE END OF THE FIRST WOE UNTO THE INHABITANTS ON THE EARTH.

CHAPTER 9

VS 1-12 THE FIFTH TRUMPET IS BLOWN AND SATAN IS CAST ONTO THE EARTH, NO LONGER HAVING ACCESS TO HEAVEN TO ACCUSE THE SAINTS DAY AND NIGHT. HE IS GIVEN THE KEY TO THE BOTTOMLESS PIT TO LOOSE DEMONISTIC CREATURES UPON THE EARTH.

VS 13-21 THE SIXTH TRUMPET IS BLOWN AND A GREAT ARMY IS LOOSED FROM THE EAST TO KILL ONE THIRD OF THE MEN ON THE EARTH IN A TERRIBLE WAR.

CHAPTER 10

VS 1-7 THERE IS A BREAK BETWEEN THE SIXTH TRUMPET AND THE SEVENTH TRUMPET WITH A STRONG ANGLE (THE LORD JESUS CHRIST) WITH A LITTLE BOOK. THE SCENE HAS CHANGED BACK TO THE EARTH.

VS 8-11 JOHN IS COMMANDED TO EAT THE LITTLE BOOK.

CHAPTER 11

VS 1-2 JOHN IS COMMANDED TO MEASURE THE TEMPLE IN JERUSALEM THAT HAS BEEN REBUILT IN WHICH THE ANTI-CHRIST RULES THE WORLD FROM FOR FORTY-TWO MONTHS (THREE AND ONE HALF YEARS).

VS 3-12 THE TWO WITNESSES PROPHESY FOR FORTY-TWO MONTHS.

VS 13-14 THERE IS A GREAT EARTHQUAKE KILLING SEVEN THOUSAND MEN. THIS IS THE END OF THE SECOND WOE UNTO THE INHABITANTS ON THE EARTH.

VS 15-19 THE SEVENTH TRUMPET IS BLOWN AND THE END TO THE TRIBULATION OF SEVEN YEARS. THE SCENE CHANGES BACK TO HEAVEN WITH THE OPENING OF THE TEMPLE IN HEAVEN.

CHAPTER 12

THERE IS A BREAK IN THE JUDGMENTS FROM CHAPTER 12 TO CHAPTER 13. JOHN SEES SEVEN PERSONALITIES AND EXPLAINS WHO THESES PERSONS ARE WHICH IS KEY TO UNDERSTANDING THE ENTIRE BOOK OF REVELATIONS.

VS 1-2 THE WOMAN IS ISRAEL.

VS 3-4 THE RED DRAGON IS SATAN.

VS 5-6 THE CHILD OF THE WOMAN IS THE LORD JESUS CHRIST.

VS 7-12 MICHAEL, THE ARCHANGEL, WARS WITH THE DRAGON.

VS 13-16 SATAN PERSECUTES THE WOMAN, BECAUSE OF THE CHILD.

VS 17 SATAN HATES THE REMNANT OF THE WOMAN AND WARS AGAINST THEM.

CHAPTER 13

WE SEE THE LAST TWO PERSONALITIES WHICH ARE REVEALED DURING THE TRIBULATION PERIOD.

VS 1-2 THE WILD BEAST THAT RISES OUT OF THE SEA WHO IS THE ANTI-CHRIST.

VS 3 THE MIRACLE OF THE WOUNDED HEAD OF THE BEAST.

VS 4-5 THE WORLD GIVES POWER UNTO THE BEAST AND THEY WORSHIP HIM AS GOD.

VS 6-8 THE BEAST DEFIES GOD AND ANYONE WHO WORSHIPS GOD.

VS 9-10 WARNING AGAINST THE WAYS OF THE BEAST.

VS 11 THE WILD BEAST OUT OF THE EARTH WHO IS THE FALSE PROPHET.

VS 12-14 THIS BEAST CAUSED THE WORLD TO WORSHIP THE FIRST BEAST.

VS 15-17 ALL MANKIND IS FORCED TO RECEIVE THE MARK OF THE FIRST BEAST AND WORSHIP HIM AS GOD.

VS 18   THE NUMBER OF THE BEAST.

CHAPTER 14

JOHN SEES THE END OF THE TRIBULATION PERIOD AND THE REMNANT OF 144,000 LIVING JEWS REMAINING ON THE EARTH.

VS 1-5 JOHN SEES THE LAMB OF GOD WITH THE 144,000 REDEEMED SAINTS WITH THE SEAL OF GOD IN THEIR FOREHEADS.

VS 6-7 THERE IS AN ANGEL THAT PROCLAIMS THE GOSPEL TO ALL ON THE EARTH THAT HAVE REJECTED THE LORD JESUS CHRIST AND THE MESSAGE OT THE TWO WITNESSES FOR FORTY-TWO MONTHS.

VS 8   A SECOND ANGEL FOLLOWS WITH THE PRONOUNCEMENT OF JUDGMENT ON THAT WICKED CITY BABYLON, WHICH IS ROME THE NEW BABYLON.

VS 9-12 A THIRD ANGLE FOLLOWS WITH THE PRONOUNCEMENT OF JUDGMENT ON ALL WHO HAVE RECEIVED THE MARK OF THE BEAST.

VS 13   THERE IS PRAISE IN HEAVEN FOR ALL WHO DIED FOR THE SAKE OF CHRIST DURING THE TRIBULATION PERIOD.

VS 14-20 JOHN SEES THE GREAT BATTLE OF ARMAGEDDON WHEN CHRIST RETURNS TO THE EARTH AS KING OF KINGS.

CHAPTER 15

THE FINAL JUDGMENTS ON THE EARTH IN CHAPTER 15 AND CHAPTER 16 WITH THE POURING OUT OF THE SEVEN BOWLS OF THE WRATH OF GOD UPON THE EARTH.

VS 1-4 THE TRIBULATIONS SAINTS PRAISE GOD BECAUSE HE IS HOLY AND TRUE. THERE IS SINGING IN HEAVEN.

VS 5-8 THE TEMPLE OF HEAVEN IS OPENED TO LET THE SEVEN ANGELS WITH THE BOWLS OF THE WRATH OF GOD COME FORTH. IN THE TEMPLE DAYS ON THE EARTH, BOWLS OF BLOOD WERE PLACED ON THE ALTAR TO ATONE FOR THE PEOPLES SINS. THERE IS NO BLOOD FOR THE INHABITANTS ON THE EARTH AND NOW BOWLS OF GODS WRATH ARE CARRIED OUT OF THE TEMPLE IN HEAVEN TO CAST ONTO THE PEOPLE ON THE EARTH.

TO THIS POINT IN THE TRIBULATION PERIOD WE HAVE SEEN:

SEVEN SEALED SCROLL:

1. RIDER ON A WHITE HORSE

2. RIDER ON RED HORSE

3. RIDER ON BLACK HORSE

4. RIDER ON PALE HORSE

5. PRAYER OF THE MARTYRED REMNANT

6. BEGINNING OF THE LAST 42 MONTHS

7. SEVENTH SEAL INTRODUCES THE SEVEN TRUMPETS

SEVEN TRUMPETS:

1. TREES ARE BURNED UP

2. SEAS BECOME BLOOD

3. FRESH WATER BECOMES WORMWOOD

4. SUN, MOON AND STARS ARE SMITTEN

5. FALLEN STAR FROM HEAVEN LETS THE LOCUST LOOSE FROM THE BOTTOMLESS PIT

6. ANGLE LOOSED AT THE RIVER EUPHRATES

7. END OF THE TRIBULATION COMES QUICKLY

SEVEN PERFORMERS OR PERSONALITIES:

1. THE WOMAN- ISRAEL

2. THE RED DRAGON- SATAN

3. THE CHILD OF THE WOMAN- CHRIST JESUS

4. MICHAEL WARS WITH SATAN

5. REMNANT OF ISRAEL - 144,000

6. THE WILD BEAST OUT OF THE SEA- THE ANTI-CHRIST

7. THE WILD BEAST OUT OF THE EARTH- THE FALSE PROPHET

THE SEVEN BOWLS OF THE WRATH OF GOD WHICH ARE POURED OUT :

CHAPTER 16

VS 1-2 FIRST BOWL POURED OUT- BOILS AND INFECTIONS ON THE PEOPLE.

VS 3 SECOND BOWL POURED OUT- ALL THE SEAS BECAME BLOOD AND ALL THAT WAS IN THE SEA DIED.

VS 4-7 THIRD BOWL POURED OUT- ALL THE FRESH WATER BECAME BLOOD.

VS 8-9 FOURTH BOWL POURED OUT- ON THE SUN TO TORMENT WITH GREAT HEAT.

VS 10-11 FIFTH BOWL POURED OUT- DARKNESS OVER THE EARTH.

VS 12 SIXTH BOWEL POURED OUT- RIVER EUPHRATES DRIED UP.

VS 13-16 THE BATTLE OF ARMAGEDDON.

VS 17-21 SEVENTH BOWL POURED OUT- IT IS DONE.

CHAPTER 17

WE SEE THE TWO BABYLON'S JUDGED IN CHAPTER 17 AND 18.

VS 1-7 THE GREAT HARLOT RIDING THE WILD BEAST- THIS BABYLON IS THE APOSTATE CHURCH REFEREED TO IN REVELATIONS 2:20-22.

VS 8-18 THE WILD BEAST DESTROYS THE GREAT HARLOT.

CHAPTER 18

VS 1-8 THIS IS THE COMMERCIAL BABYLON DESTROYED BY GOD.

VS 9-19 THE ANGUISH OF THE WORLD OVER THE DESTRUCTION OF COMMERCIAL BABYLON.

VS 20-24 ANTICIPATION OF JOY IN HEAVEN BECAUSE OF THE DESTRUCTION OF COMMERCIAL BABYLON.

CHAPTER 19

"AFTER THESE THINGS" AFTER THE DESTRUCTION OF THE RELIGIOUS BABYLON AND THE COMMERCIAL BABYLON THE LORD IS READY TO RETURN TO THE EARTH.

VS 1-6 HEAVEN SINGS "ALLELUIA" - PRAISE THE LORD.

VS 7-10 THE MARRIAGE OF THE LAMB OF GOD WITH HIS BRIDE (HIS CHURCH).

VS 11-16 THE RETURN OF CHRIST AS "KING OF KINGS AND LORD OF LORDS"

VS 17-19 THE BATTLE OF ARMAGEDDON.

VS 20-21 HELL IS OPENED AND THE FALSE PROPHET AND THE ANTI-CHRIST ARE CAST INTO HELL AS THE FIRST INHABITANTS OF GEHENNA

1. HADES
2. GEHENNA
3. THE BOTTOMLESS PIT

CHAPTER 20

THE MILLENNIUM (THOUSAND YEAR REIGN OF CHRIST AS KING OF KINGS AND LORD OF LORDS) THE MILLENNIUM CAN NOT OCCUR UNTIL THESE THINGS HAVE HAPPENED.

1. SATAN IS REMOVED AND CAST INTO THE BOTTOMLESS PIT.

2. THE CURSE OF SIN IS REMOVED ISAIAH 11:6-9, 35:1-10, ROMANS 8:18-23.

3. THE RESURRECTION OF THE TRIBULATION SAINTS TO RULE AND REIGN WITH THE LORD JESUS CHRIST WITH THE RAPTURED SAINTS THAT WILL RETURN WITH THE LORD AS "KING OF KINGS AND LORD OF LORDS" .

4. MAN WILL LIVE UNDER IDEAL CONDITIONS WHERE THE BABY CAN PLAY WITH THE VENOMOUS SNAKE AND NOT BE HARMED AND THE LAMB WILL LIE DOWN WITH THE LION TO REST.

VS 1-3 SATAN IS BOUND FOR A THOUSAND YEARS AND CAST INTO THE BOTTOMLESS PIT.

VS 4-6 THE SAINTS WILL REIGN WITH CHRIST FOR A THOUSAND YEARS.

VS 7-9 SATAN IS LOOSED FROM THE BOTTOMLESS PIT AT THE END OF THE THOUSAND YEARS FOR A SHORT TIME.

VS 10 SATAN IS CAST INTO THE LAKE OF FIRE (GEHENNA) WITH THE FALSE PROPHET AND THE ANTI-CHRIST FOR ETERNITY.

VS 11-15 SETTING OF THE GREAT WHITE THRONE WHERE ALL THE LOST ARE JUDGED AND ARE CAST INTO THE LAKE OF FIRE (GEHENNA) WITH SATAN AND HIS ANGELS.

CHAPTER 21

ETERNITY IS REVEALED WITH THE NEW HEAVEN AND THE NEW EARTH.

VS 1-2 THE NEW HEAVEN, THE NEW EARTH AND THE NEW JERUSALEM.

VS 3-8 A NEW ERA IN ETERNITY.

VS 9-21 THE NEW JERUSALEM WHICH IS THE HOME OF THE BRIDE.

VS 22-23 THE NEW RELATIONSHIP GOD DWELLS WITH THE SON AND HIS BRIDE.

VS 24-27 THE NEW CENTER OF THE NEW CREATION.

SOME OF THE CHANGES FROM THE OLD TO THE NEW:

1. THERE WILL BE NO SIN IN THE NEW

2. THE NEW JERUSALEM IS THE CENTER OF THE NEW UNIVERSE

3. THERE WILL BE TRAVEL BETWEEN THE NEW EARTH AND THE NEW JERUSALEM.

4. THERE WILL BE NO SUN FOR CHRIST WILL BE THE LIGHT OF THIS WORLD AND THERE WILL BE NO DARKNESS OR NIGHT.

5. THERE WILL BE NO SEA ON THE NEW EARTH.

6. CHRIST AND GOD WILL DWELL WITH THE BRIDE FOR EVER.

CHAPTER 22

ETERNITY IS UNVEILED

VS 1-5 THE RIVER OF LIFE AND THE TREE OF LIFE.

VS 6-16 THE PROMISE OF CHRIST RETURN AS HE SAID HE WILL.

VS 17-19 FINAL INVITATION AND WARNING FOR THOSE WHO DO NOT REPENT.

VS 20-21 FINAL PROMISE OF CHRIST RETURN AND THE SAINTS LOOKING FOR HIS RETURN AND PRAYER OF JOHN.

MOORE ABOUT REVELATION

TABLE OF EVENTS

	FIRST	SECOND	THIRD	FOURTH	FIFTH	SIXTH	SEVENTH
7 SEALS	RIDER ON THE WHITE HORSE	RIDER ON THE RED HORSE	RIDER ON THE BLACK HORSE	RIDER ON THE PALE HORSE	WHITE ROBES GIVEN TO THOSE UNDER THE ALTAR	EARTH-QUAKE SUN WAS BLACK STARS FALL ON EARTH HEAVEN DEPARTED AS A SCROLL	SILENCE IN HEAVEN BURNED INCENSE ON ALTAR SEVEN TRUMPETS GIVEN TO ANGELS
7 TRUMPETS	HAIL AND FIRE MINGLED W/ BLOOD 1/3 ALL TREES AND GRASS IS BURNED UP	GREAT MOUNTAIN OF FIRE CAST INTO SEA 1/3 ALL SEAS BECOMES BLOOD	GREAT BURNING STAR FROM HEAVEN 1/3 ALL FRESH WATER BECOMES BITTER	1/3 SUN, MOON AND STARS SHOWN DURING A DAY	STAR FALL FROM HEAVEN, HE IS GIVEN KEY TO BOTTOM-LESS PIT LOCUST BEAST HURT MEN FOR 5 MONTHS	FOUR ANGEL STOP THE RIVER EUPHRATES AND IS DRIED UP 2,000,000 MAN ARMY FROM EAST 1/3 ALL MEN KILLED IN WAR	TEMPLE IN HEAVEN OPENED LIGHTNING, THUNDER AND EARTH-QUAKE AND GREAT HAIL
7 PERSONS	WOMAN CLOTHED WITH SUN, MOON AND STARS GREAT WITH CHILD	GREAT RED DRAGON W/ SEVEN HEADS, TEN HORNS AND TEN CROWNS HIS TAIL DREW 1/3 OF STARS OF HEAVEN AND CAST THEM TO EARTH	THE MAN CHILD BORN TO THE WOMAN AND CAUGHT UP TO HEAVEN WOMAN FLED INTO WILDER-NESS FOR 42 MONTHS	WAR IN HEAVEN RED DRAGON AND MICHAEL W/ HIS ANGELS SATAN AND HIS ANGELS CAST OUT OF HEAVEN	SATAN PERSECUTES THE WOMAN WHO IS GIVEN TWO WINGS OF AN EAGLE TO FLY TO WILDERNESS AND PROTECTED FOR 42 MONTHS	BEAST OUT OF THE SEA WORSHIPPED AS GOD HAS SEVEN HEADS, TEN HORNS AND TEN CROWNS ONE HEAD IS WOUNDED AND THEN HEALED	BEAST OUT OF THE EARTH W/ TWO HORNS CAUSED EARTH TO WORSHIP FIRST BEAST CAUSED MEN TO RECEIVE MARK OF BEAST
7 THUNDERS	?	?	?	?	?	?	?
7 BOWLS OF PLAGUES	GRIEVOUS SORES ON THOSE WHO WEAR THE MARK OF THE BEAST	ALL THE SEAS BECAME AS BLOOD AND ALL CREATURES DIED IN SEA	ALL FRESH WATER BECAME BLOOD	SUN SCORCHES MEN W/ GREAT HEAT	DARKNESS ON THE SEAT OF THE BEAST AND GREAT PAIN AND SORES	RIVER EUPHRATES DRIED UP AND ALL ARMIES CONVERGE ON VALLEY OF ARMAGEDDON	GREAT EARTH-QUAKE ALL ISLANDS SINK, ALL MOUNTAINS FALL AND GREAT HAIL
THREE WOES					1 ST WOE	2 ND WOE	3 RD WOE

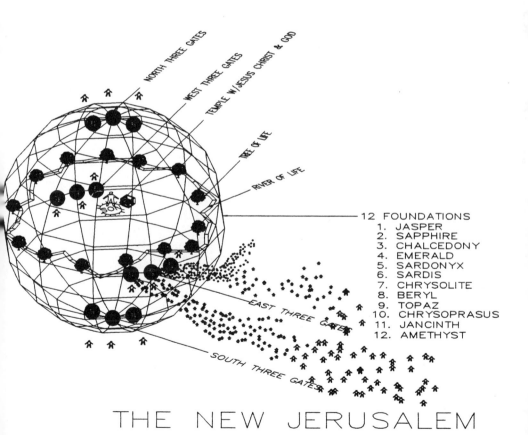

THE NEW JERUSALEM

NORTH THREE GATES

WEST THREE GATES

TEMPLE W/JESUS CHRIST & GOD

TREE OF LIFE

RIVER OF LIFE

12 FOUNDATIONS
1. JASPER
2. SAPPHIRE
3. CHALCEDONY
4. EMERALD
5. SARDONYX
6. SARDIS
7. CHRYSOLITE
8. BERYL
9. TOPAZ
10. CHRYSOPRASUS
11. JANCINTH
12. AMETHYST

EAST THREE GATES

SOUTH THREE GATES

THE NEW EARTH

INTRODUCTION

The reader of this book must look into the future and see that the end of time is closer today than when John penned this revelation given to him by Jesus some 1900 years ago. I have always been fascinated with the book of Revelation since my early faith in Jesus Christ as my Lord and Savior. In my twenties I began to study the Bible in depth. My becoming a Sunday school teacher required me to study and to dig into the Bible to know what I was teaching to my class. In my thirties God called me to join a church that taught the Bible and the people had a hunger for the Word of God. I surrendered to the calling of being an assistant lay pastor of this church with the pastor giving me the opportunity to preach in the church and to lead a regular Bible study at a large twelve story apartment building for the elderly. I meet with these elderly saints of God once a week and led them in verse by verse studies through the Bible. After some eight years of studying, teaching Sunday school, teaching training union, preaching in my own church, and every Tuesday night at the housing for the elderly, I had studied on an average some twenty hours a week. I kept outlines of every book of the Bible that I taught with other studies from correspondence schools, books and commentaries that I read. This study has given me a love for the book of Revelation and an understanding of John's symbolism and connection to the entire Bible. I feel that this information may help you in your desire to understand the book of Revelation better.

Being a professional Architect also has caused me to look at what makes this world what it is. I take peoples ideas and incorporate them into tangible designs and drawings that can be read to build the intricate parts of a structure into what services the

1

inhabitants of these buildings. I feel that this gift of seeing things in my mind and transposing them to tangible paper and ink representations has also enabled me to read the book of Revelation and see to some part what John was seeing some 1900 years ago. Today, of course, it is easier to understand most of what a man living in the first century tried to convey in words when he had never seen a car or an airplane. Even Bible scholars just fifty years ago would not understand a lot of what John was writing about.

I hope you will read this book with the same desire to understand God's Word and come to the same understanding that we live in the end of times referred to by the apostles when Jesus shall return for his bride, the church or more accurately those that believe in the Lord Jesus Christ as their savior, and this earth is plunged into seven years of tribulation.

I like to refer to the time table that God set for us in the beginning when He created this world that we live in. God created this earth in six days and then He rested on the seventh day from His labors. In my study of the Bible I have calculated that there were about two thousand years between the creation of Adam to the time of the flood, when God delivered Noah and his family from the flood in the Arch. There were also approximately two thousand years from the flood to the coming of Jesus Christ to this earth. There has been almost two thousand years since Christ to this present day. This adds up to almost six thousand years. The number of man is six, because he was created on the sixth day. God rested on the seventh day which is the number of completion. The Bible says in II Peter 3:1-18 **"one day is with the Lord as a thousand years, and a**

thousand years as one day." This verse gives us a key to understanding God's timetable from the beginning of time to the end of time.

		Christ Jesus	second coming	end of
Adam	the flood	was born	Christ Jesus	this world

```
+----------------------+---------------------------+------------------------+---------------------+----------------------+
```

2,000 years	2,000 years	2,000 years	1,000 years
two days	four days	six days	the seventh day

Also the final rule of Christ Jesus as Lord of Lords and King of Kings on this earth for a thousand years is referred to as "the day of rest." Now if God created this earth in six days and rested on the seventh day maybe the timetable of man on this earth is six days or six thousand years and then the day of rest with the Lord Jesus Christ is a thousand years. Every day we get closer to the year 2000. I am not predicting that Jesus will come then, but that Jesus can come at any time and that the time of his coming is closer than it was in the day that John penned this great book of Revelation.

In Luke 17:25-30 it is said by Jesus himself that as it were in the days of Sodom when perversion was so prevalent and as it were in the days of Noah when people were living a wicked life style, that it will be the same when Jesus shall come again to this earth. I pray that you read this book and receive the blessing and knowledge of what

3

Jesus has done for you and I on the cross of Calvary when He died in our place and took our punishment on himself for our sins. Jesus also rose again from the grave on the third day, victorious over death, with the promise to all that trust in Him shall receive a resurrected body just like His when he comes again.

MOORE ABOUT REVELATION

REVELATION CHAPTER 1

The word revelation means the revealing of something that has been hidden. This book reveals Jesus to us as the King of Kings and Lord of Lords coming back to this earth some day in judgment over the wicked that have rejected Him as their savior. Many churches today teach about the love of Jesus and fail to teach about the judgment of Jesus that will fall on all the unbelievers. This books purpose is show unto his servants things which must shortly come to pass.

John was about 95 years old when he was exiled to the little island of Patmos by the Roman Caesar Domitian. The Roman Caesar by that time was worshipped as a god by the people of the Roman Empire and their hatred of Christians was carried out through sport in the arenas in Rome. During the tribulation period that John reveals to us, I believe that the world will be much like the early church days where the anti-christ will persecute those who worship Jesus Christ. During the tribulation period a one world religion will be forced on all the world with the anti-Christ being the one worshipped and exhalted above all other religions. With the rebirth of the Roman Empire during the tribulation period, the anti-christ will exhalt himself as God just like the Roman caesar Domitian during the time that John was exhiled to Patmos. John was put on this island to die, because he would not stop preaching about Jesus Christ, but he lived and God used John to record one of the most important books of our New Testament.

Vs 1 **"The Revelation of Jesus Christ, which God gave unto him, to show unto his servants things which must shortly come to pass: and he sent and signified it by his angel unto his servant John."**

This revealing to John comes from Jesus himself, who is relaying His Fathers message about the future events in time. The key to what Jesus is going to reveal to John and what he is to write about is found in verse 19 of this chapter: 1) things which thou hast seen 2) things which are and 30 things which shall be hereafter. John also is told that these things must shortly come to pass. If time was short when John penned this book, then it must be the eleventh hour by now for these things that Jesus reveals to John to come to pass. John calls himself a servant of Jesus Christ. Literally a bond servant as one who has served his time under his master and paid the debt he owed, but because he loved his master he continues serving his master. This is the only kind of service that is acceptable to the Lord Jesus as recorded by Paul in I Corinthians 13: 1-13 **"and now abideth faith, hope, charity (love), these three; but the greatest of these is charity."** What is revealed to John must shortly come to pass, just as sure to happen as if it already had.

Vs 2 **"Who bare record of the Word of God, and of the testimony of Jesus Christ, and of all things that he saw."**

John bears record of four things. 1) he bears record of the Word of God or the scriptures or the Old Testament, which is all that they had at this time. 2) he bears record of the living Word of Jesus himself and his life on this earth for John had seen the sinless perfect life of Jesus on this earth. 3) he bears record of the testimony of Jesus Word and his teaching the apostles in the way that we should live our lives on this earth. 4) he bears record of all things that he saw

Jesus perform and the countless miracles and healing of all ailments known to man in that day. The ultimate miracle was even raising the dead to life again. Only by the power of God could a man do these things, thus validating his claim to being the very son of God.

Vs 3   **"Blessed is he that readeth, and they that hear the words of this prophecy, and keep those things which are written therein: for the time is at hand."**

There are three groups of people who will be blessed. 1) he that readeth this book. 2) he that heareth the words of this book read. 3) he that applies the things that he has heard and reads from this book to living his life looking for the Lord Jesus to come again as if it were today. Every day a Christian should live his life as if Jesus were coming that day and time was short for doing the things needed doing for the sake of our Lord.

Seven is a divine number, a complete number, a number of perfection. The number of churches that John is commanded to write to is no accident. I believe that these churches were in existence when John wrote the book to them, but the content and the sequence of the order they are in is of utmost importance. We are living in what is called the Church Age, when Jesus is calling out a bride or saved ones to call up to be with him in eternity. I believe that these letters to the seven churches represent seven church ages that will finally end when the Lord Jesus comes back to this earth as King of Kings and Lord of Lords to rule and reign on this earth with his church for a thousand years. Looking back into the history of the church on this earth since Jesus was crucified on the cross of Calvary to this present day we can see many of the very things that John records in each letter to these different churches and attribute them to different ages in time. I will try to point this out as we read the letters to the seven churches.

Vs 4 **"John to the seven churches which are in Asia: Grace be unto you, and peace, from Him which is, and which was, and which is to come; and from the seven Spirits which are before his throne."**

Grace and peace be unto you is a common greeting from a Christian to another Christian and was used in the opening words in almost all of the books of Paul. This shows the love in Johns heart and his desire for Jesus to bless the fellow Christians that John is writing to. In that day of persecution against Christians by the Romans and the Jews, all Christians needed the grace of God and the peace of Jesus Christ to live day by day. Jesus promised to give us peace that passeth all understanding by the world around us if we just ask him for it. This is what causes the unsaved world around us to wonder how we can go on each day with our lives when it seems that the world is falling down around us. When others curse and vent anger in their troubled lives, a Christian can just keep on smiling and trust in God to provide grace and Jesus to give us a peace that calms all our fears. John sends the wishes if grace and peace from He who sits on the throne in heaven. 1) He who is at the very moment John is writing this book. 2) He who was from the beginning of time even when God created this universe and created Adam and Eve. 3) He who is to come according to the promises of this book that John is recording.

Vs 5   **"And from Jesus Christ, who is the faithful witness, and the first begotten of the dead, and the prince of the kings of the earth. Unto him that loved us, and washed us from our sins in his own blood."**

Who is this grace and peace from that John sends to the readers and hearers of this book: 1) Jesus Christ who is the faithful witness, even unto death on the cross of Calvary, Jesus was faithful to God's will to provide the sacrifice for the sins of the world. 2) Jesus Christ who was the first begotten of the dead, to reveal to all men and women who trust in him as their Lord and Savior that we to are promised a ever-living eternal body just like his. 3) Jesus Christ the prince of the kings of earth, there being none fairer, none exhalted higher than he, none to compare with he. 4) Jesus Christ that loved us and gave himself to be crucified and shed his perfect sinless blood on the cross of Calvary so that we could be set free from the penalty of sin, eternal death.

Vs 6   **"And hath made us kings and priest unto God and his Father; to him be glory and dominion for ever and ever. Amen."**

We as Christians see our position in Christ Jesus in this world. We shall inherit the earth, our riches do not even compare with the worlds things. How can one put a value on eternal life and the love of Jesus Christ, when the lost world thinks that this worlds things are what make one wealthy. We are made priest unto God in Christ Jesus. We do not need an earthly priest to intercede for us like the high priest in the Temple in Jerusalem, who year by year took the blood of bulls and goats as a sacrifice into the holy of holies to make restitution for the sins of the people. When Christ Jesus died on the cross of Calvary the veil separating the holy of holies from the people and the altar where the sacrifices were taken in by the high priest, was torn from corner to corner, opening the way for all to have access unto God's holy altar to receive forgiveness. Our high priest is now Jesus Christ who takes our prayers directly to the Father to intercede for us in our hour of need. Hebrews 7: 19-28. 9:1-14. Positionally we are all priest, now in Jesus Christ, who can take our petitions directly to the altar of God any time of the day and night through our Lord Jesus Christ and the Holy Spirit. Romans 8:24-27.

Vs 7 **"Behold, he cometh with clouds; and every eye shall see him, and they also which pierced him: and all kindreds of the earth shall wail because of him. Even so, A-men."**

In Luke 21: 25-28 Jesus himself tells us that he shall return in a cloud and gives signs of the time when he shall come again. Acts 1: 9-11 records that Jesus left this earth in a cloud and two angles told the apostles who witnessed his ascension, that this same Jesus will return in like manner as they have seen him go into heaven. When Jesus does come back to this earth at the end of the tribulation period, every eye shall see him. John did not say some, but every eye, even those that pierced him. I believe that even the windows of hell will be flung open to show them the return of Jesus Christ to this earth, even those men that crucified our Lord Jesus Christ on the cross of Calvary and pierced his side to prove that he was dead. The inhabitants on the earth at the end of the tribulation period are all going to see Jesus when he comes in a cloud back to this earth. John sees them wailing at his return, knowing that it is over for them and the final judgment is waiting for them. John adds an A-men "even so, let it be true."

Vs 8   **"I am Alpha and Omega, the beginning and the ending, saith the Lord, which is, and which was, and which is to come, the Almighty."**

Jesus is the beginning and the end. Jesus was with God when the earth was created. I John 1:1 **"That which was from the beginning, which we have heard, which we have seen with our own eyes, which we have looked upon, and our hands have handled, of the Word of life;"** Jesus reaches all the way back to the creation and then all the way to the end of this earth into eternity. Jesus is present, past and future, the Almighty God of this world.

Vs 9   **"I John, who also am your brother, and companion in tribulation, and in the kingdom and patience of Jesus Christ, was in the isle that is called Patmos, for the word of God, and for the testimony of Jesus Christ."**

John identifies himself as the writer as a sufferer also in the tribulation for the cause of Jesus Christ on this earth, as a brother with all the believers and Christians. John may be saying to all of us that if we stand for the cause of Jesus Christ, we must endure the suffering and have patience looking for Christ to come some day. In Romans 8:18-23 Paul tells us **"For we know that the whole** creation groaneth and travaileth in pain together until now. And not only they, but ourselves also, which have the first fruits of the Spirit, even we ourselves groan within ourselves, waiting for the adoption, to wit, the redemption of our body." John was exhiled to this rocky little island, literally to die there, for his preaching and giving his testimony for Jesus Christ.

Vs 10 **"I was in the Spirit on the Lord's day, and heard behind me a great voice as of a trumpet,"**

The Sabbath was the day of worship under the law, and the first day of the week was the day that the Lord Jesus rose from the dead which was referred to as the Lord's day. I Corinthians 16: 1-2 and Acts Chapter 2. John referred to the first day of the week as the Lord's day. In the Old Testament days the trumpet was used to announce the coming of the king, or an important message was about to be heard. The voice of Jesus was like a trumpet sounding.

Vs 11 **"Saying, I am Alpha and Omega, the first and the last: and, what thou seest, write in a book, and send it unto the seven churches which are in Asia; unto Ephesus, and unto Pergamos, and unto Thyatira, and unto Sardis, and unto Smyrna, and unto Philadelphia, and unto Laodicea."**

Jesus calls himself the first and the last, or the beginning and the end. Jesus was in the beginning when God created the heavens and the earth and he will be at the end when this world as we know it now will end, and Jesus creates the new heavens and the new earth for eternity. John is commissioned to write what he sees into a book and to send it to the churches that he calls out. The number of churches is seven and is not to missed as to the importance of order. I will discuss this importance as we go.

Vs 12 **"And I turned to see the voice that spake with me. And being turned, I saw seven golden candlesticks;"**

The explanation of the seven candlesticks is given by Jesus in Vs 20. John describes seven traits of our Lord Jesus that he saw as he looked upon this one who stands in the midst of the seven candlesticks. John is looking on Christ Jesus now as the one who now coming as the judge of this world.

Vs 13 **"And in the midst of the seven candlesticks one like unto the Son of man, clothed with a garment down to the foot, and a girt about his paps with a golden girdle."**

Fist trait: Jesus has a golden girdle around his breast or "paps." Gold is a symbol or righteousness. He will not change, he is the same Jesus that came to save the world. Hebrews 13:8 **"Jesus the same yesterday, today and tomorrow."** All the gold that was placed on this earth is still here, except for the gold that maybe flying around this earth in satellites. Gold will not rust or decompose, it is the same today as it was in the beginning.

Vs 14 **"His head and his hairs were white like wool, as white as snow; and his eyes were as a flame of fire;"**

Second trait: Jesus hair was white ad snow and white like wool. White hair on the head symbolizes maturity of age, wisdom of authority and purity as the new snow.

Third trait: Jesus eyes were like a flame of fire, with nothing escaping his gaze. Jesus eyes see into the very soul of man to reveal even the inner most thoughts. Like a fire burns away all that hides the inner most part of our being. Latter on we will see that when the saved stand before Jesus at the "Bema" or judgment seat of Jesus to receive rewards for the way we lived on this earth, his eyes burn away the works of wood, hay and stubble, but the works of gold, silver and precious stones will be refined even purer and more brilliant than before.

Vs 15 **"And his feet like unto fine brass, as if they burned in a furnace; and his voice as the sound of many waters."**

Fourth trait: Jesus feet were like fine brass or bronze, as if they burned or glowed with heat like a furnace. Brass symbolizes judgment in the bible. Exodus 30 describes the laver and its feet were made of brass and was filled with water to wash the hands and the feet of those who entered into the Ark of the Covenant to offer the sacrifices unto the Lord God. If the priest did not wash his feet or his hands then he would die, for the judgment of God would fall on them.

Fifth trait: Jesus voice was like the sound of many waters. Have you ever stood near a large water fall? Niagara has a thundering sound that deafens those who stand there. When Jesus comes again, his voice commands authority and the listeners must hear what he is saying. Jesus speaks today to the people through the voice of his preachers and the saints to the world, but they are to busy to hear, or just turn away. In that day when Jesus comes as judge over this world all will hear him, but it will be to late.

Vs 16 **"And he had in his right hand seven stars: and out of his mouth went a sharp two-edged sword: and his countenance was as the sun shineth in his strength."**

The seven stars in Jesus right hand will be explained in Vs 20.

Sixth trait: Out of Jesus mouth proceedeth a sharp two-edged sword. Ephesians 6:17 **"And take the helmet of salvation, and the sword of the Spirit, which is the word of God."** Hebrews 4:12 **"For the word of God is quick, and powerful, and sharper than any two-edged sword, piercing even to the dividing asunder of soul and spirit, and of the joints and marrow, and is a discerner of the thoughts and intents of the heart."** The word of God is more powerful than any thing on this earth or in the devil's spirit world. We should use the word of God (the Bible) to combat Satan and his attacks on our lives. When Jesus was tested in the desert by Satan, Jesus resisted every temptation by quoting scripture back to him and there was no reply to the word of God by Satan.

Seventh trait: Jesus countenance was like the sun in the strongest part of the day. Jesus called himself the light of the world. In fact when we get to the creation of the new heaven and the new earth, Jesus will be the light of the eternal new heaven and new earth. When the church and the Holy Spirit are taken out of this earth at the rapture, the darkness that will be left on this earth will be so horrible, for there will not be any saved that can restrain Satan and his anti-Christ from totally dominating this earth for seven years.

Vs 17 **"And when I saw him, I fell at his feet as dead. And he laid his right hand upon me, saying unto me, Fear not: I am the first and the last:"**

Can you just imagine the emotions of John just ran away with him and he fainted at the sight of his Lord and Savior Jesus Christ.

Vs 18 **"I am He that liveth, and was dead; and behold, I am alive for evermore, A-men; and have the keys to hell and of death."**

Jesus reassures John that it is Jesus himself, and not to fear, for he is there to strengthen him, and raises John back to his feet. Many churches teach that a man on this earth has the keys to hell to excommunicate men to eternal judgment in hell, and theses keys are passed from Pope to Pope. If you will notice who has the keys in this verse.

Vs 19 **"Write the things which thou hast seen, and the things which are, and the things which shall be hereafter."**

John is commanded to write about three things: 1) the things he has seen or the accounts of Jesus life. 2) the things which are or at that time that John lived. 3) and the things which shall be hereafter, which John is about to see about the future.

Vs 20 **"The mystery of the seven stars which thou sawest in my right hand, and the seven golden candlesticks. The seven stars are the angels of the seven churches: and the seven candlesticks which thou sawest are the seven churches."**

The Churches today that are following the Lord Jesus Christ and fulfilling the great commission of the Lord Jesus, going into all the world teaching and baptizing the lost in the name of Jesus, are in the right hand of Jesus and the gates of hell cannot prevail against them. Jesus tells John that the stars in his right hand are the angel or pastors of his churches and the golden candlesticks that John saw are the seven churches that Jesus commands John to write this book to. If we are in the right hand of Jesus, then who can pluck us out of his hand? We should rest assured that as long as we are doing the will of Jesus Christ that no one will be able to harm our eternal soul, for we are in his hand of mercy. The world may kill this body that we live in, but the assurance of our salvation is in the right hand of Jesus himself.

REVELATION CHAPTER 2

The first part of the vision deals with the Church Age. The second part of the vision starts in Chapter 4, where the vision changes from the earthly to a vision of Glory. The first part of the vision deals with the letters to the seven churches where John is being told what to write by Jesus Christ who stands in the midst of the seven candlesticks, or seven churches as indicated in Chapter 1:20. The second part of the vision is a picture of the glorified church or those taken to Heaven in the rapture. Between the two visions the rapture has taken place, when Christ Jesus Christ comes in the air and calls all those who have trusted in Jesus as their Lord and Savior; I Thessalonians 4:14-18. After the rapture of the saints or the Church then the tribulation period begins and last for seven years. The judgment on those who are left on the earth begins in Chapter 6 through Chapter 19, and then the King of Kings comes back to the earth with the glorified saints to rule and reign over this earth for 1,000 years.

Some churches teach that the church will go through one half or even all of the tribulation. The Bible tells us **"So as it were in the days of Noah so shall it be in the days of the coming of the Son of Man."** Not one drop of water fell until all the animals and Noah's family were sealed up in the Ark by God. No judgment fell on the righteous. Scripture tells us also **"As it were in the days of Sodom and Gohoroma so shall it be in the days of the coming of the Son of Man."** God sent two angels into the city to take Lot and his family out of the city before any fire and brimstone fell on that wicked city. The church will not go through the tribulation period. The saints are pictured around the throne of God as the seals and trumpet judgments are placed upon the inhabitants on the earth that are left after the rapture of the church.

I believe that the letters to the seven churches represent seven church ages, which can be seen as you look into the history of the church. The book of Revelations is prophetic of what is to come as Jesus told John. These letters also apply to all the churches through out the church age and should be applied us today as well.

LETTER TO CHURCH AT EPHESUS

The letter to the first church at Ephesus, I believe is the Apostolic age to the time that John lived in 90 AD. The city at Ephesus was the capital of idolatry and the very famous Temple of Diana was located there.

Vs 1   **"Unto the angel of the church of Ephesus write; These things saith he that holdeth the seven stars in his right hand, who walketh in the midst of the seven golden candlesticks:"**

The angel of the church as Chapter 1:20 tells us is one of the seven stars that Jesus holds in his right hand. This is the pastor of the Church at Ephesus which is one of the seven candlesticks. Angel means messenger of God and the Pastor is the messenger to the church at Ephesus. John is told to write this letter to the pastor of the church at Ephesus.

<u>Vs 2</u> **"I know thy works, and thy labor, and thy patience, and how thou cants not bear them which are evil: and thou hast tried them which say they are apostles, and are not, and hast found them liars:"**

Jesus knows their works and their labors. This church must have been doing something right! Also they had patience, which tells me that they also endured tribulation. Romans 5:1-5 tells us that we should glory in tribulation knowing that tribulation teaches us patience, and patience teaches us through experience, and experience teaches us to put our hope in Jesus Christ and his coming again to take us out of this world, and not put our hope in the things of this world like the unsaved. The more tribulation we endure the more patience we will have. Have you ever prayed for patience? You are praying for more tribulation for tribulation builds our patience.

The early church at Ephesus, during the apostles days had many Judaisers come in teaching their doctrine of a mixture of faith in Christ Jesus and works under the law of the Jews for salvation. This was common throughout the early church, as John and other preachers traveled from church to church, these men followed behind them trying to add onto what the apostles had taught in the churches. I John 4:1-6 tells us about these men who preached anything other than faith in Jesus Christ for salvation, then he is anti-Christ. This church tried these false apostles to see if what they preached was true and found them liars. If a man of God teaches the true Word of God, then he will not teach anything that disagrees with God's Word.

Vs 3   **"And hast borne, and hast patience, and for my name's sake hast labored, and hast not fainted."**

There are just a few people in our churches today that do the work and labor for the cause of Christ. There are just a few who go out soul winning and help the pastor to lead the church. Most just come on Sunday and go home, and leave the work to the pastor because he is being paid to do it. In this church at Ephesus, most of the people were working for the cause of Jesus. Today a new convert comes into our church and we load them down with things to do and then leave to do it alone. They become weary and faint most of the time, and give up. This church is commended for not fainting. There is a difference in being weary of the work and being weary doing the work.

Vs 4   **"Nevertheless I have somewhat against thee, because thou hast left thy first love."**

They were commended for things, but they were not perfect. Like a marriage between a man and his wife. In the beginning a couple is on fire with love for each other, and as the years go by sometimes that love diminishes and after a while that love that burned so bright just dies. A real love between man and his wife as the years go by will get stronger and stronger, as it should in any marriage where there is real love and not just sex to hold them together. Jesus, I believe is saying here that that love for him by this church was on fire at one time, and now it has dwindled down to a flickering flame compared to what they had for him at one time.

Vs 5 **"Remember therefore from whence thou art fallen, and repent, and do the first works; or else I will come unto thee quickly, and will remove thy candlestick out of his place, except thou repent."**

This church was going backwards instead of forward in their love for the cause of Christ and needed to repent. Every believer needs to repent of their sins, and want to get right back in love with Jesus. This should be a daily thing for us, to repent from the things that hinder us from serving Jesus in the work of the church. What was their first works? Taking the Gospel into the world is the work of the church, and I believe this is where they were falling backwards and not doing. Jesus says that he will remove the candlestick out of his place if they do not repent. Jesus will remove the church if they fail to repent. Paul established this church on his third missionary journey through Asia Minor, and John was the pastor of this church latter on. John was exhiled to the island of Patmos, I believe for pastoring this church, and latter returned to this church where he pastored to his death. The Basilica to St. John was built over his grave at Ephesus.

Ephesus was a very pagan area where the largest pagan temple in all Asia was built to Diana, the goddess of love. This temple had beautiful green marble columns which were taken by Justianian to build Haggis Sofia in Istanbul. In 256

AD Ephesus was destroyed by the Goof's, and until the early 1900's an English archeologist unearthed the buried city. Jesus may have allowed this city to be destroyed because they did not repent.

Vs 6 **"But this thou hast, that hatest the deeds of the Nicolaitans, which I also hate."**

This church at Ephesus has some good things going for them, that they hated the deeds of the Nicolaitans. "Nikao" means to conquer or rule over, and "Laos" means laity or common people of the church or the membership. This is the time when the high priestly order began to rule over the common people of the church. Not all people were not equal as believers in Jesus Christ. I Timothy 2:5 **"For there is one God, and one mediator between God and men, the man Christ Jesus."** Jesus also hated the deeds of the Nicolaitans in his church.

Vs 7 **"He that hath an ear, let him hear what the Spirit saith unto the churches: To him that overcometh will I give to eat of the tree of life, which is in the midst of the paradise of God."**

Eternal life comes only from Jesus Christ and he grants eternal life to those that call upon his name and ask Jesus to forgive them of their sins, repenting from serving sin in their lives and surrendering to the Holy Spirit to serve Jesus Christ. Jesus calls this change in a persons life as being born again. John 3:3-16 (Please read this scripture) Jesus told Nicodemus **"Except a man be born again, he cannot see the kingdom of God."** Nicodemus could not understand how he could be born twice. Jesus said **"Verily, verily, I say unto thee, Except a man be born of water and of Spirit, he cannot enter into the kingdom of God. That which is born of flesh is flesh; and that which is born of Spirit is spirit. And as Moses lifted up the serpent in the wilderness, even so must the Son of man be lifted up: That whosoever believeth in him should not perish, but have eternal life. For God so loved the world, that he gave his only begotten Son, that whosoever believeth in him should not perish, but have everlasting life."** In order to born again, a person must be born of water and spirit. Ephesians 5:26 **"That he might sanctify it (his church) with the washing of water by the Word."** Being born again by water and the Spirit. What do we base our faith on in Jesus Christ, is it not the Bible or the Word of God that tells us about his Son from Geneses to Revelations. Believing the Word of God and receiving the Holy Spirit is why Jesus gives us eternal life. Romans 3:23 **"For all have sinned, and come short of the glory of God." Romans 5:12 "Wherefore, as by one man sin entered into the world, and death by sin; and so death passed upon all men, for that all have sinned."** Romans 6:23 **"For the wages of sin is death; but the gift of God is eternal life through Jesus Christ our Lord." Romans 5:8 "But God commendeth his love toward us, in that , while we were yet sinners, Christ died for us."** Romans 10:9-13 **"That if thou shalt confess with thy mouth the Lord Jesus, and shalt believe in thine heart that God hath raised him from the dead, thou shalt be saved. For with the heart man believeth unto righteousness; and with the mouth confession is** made unto salvation. **For the scriptures saith, whosoever believeth on him (Jesus) shall not be ashamed. For whosoever shall call upon the name of the Lord shall be saved."** You can have head knowledge of what Jesus did on the Cross for us, but without heart knowledge there is no repentance from sin. The heart is what we call the seat of our emotions, where we are moved emotionally by some sad story or happy occasion. When our heart is broken by what Jesus did for us on the cross, giving his every thing, life, body and Soul so I can be saved, then I confess with my mouth, that I am a sinner, condemned to go to hell, and put my trust in his Word and ask Jesus to forgive me, then I am born again. Our nature is changed from continually wanting to get into sin, to continually wanting to serve Christ and not sinning. It's like the pig and cat nature. You can take a pig and clean him up, put a pretty pink bow on his head, and parade him up and down the church aisles, but when you turn him loose into the barn yard, He will find the first big mud hole and bury up to his nose in it. The cat nature, on the other hand is like a truly born again Christian. When the cat gets into the barn yard, he tries to walk around all the mud holes, and if he does step into one, then he licks the mud off his paws and cleans himself up. A truly born again Christian will fall into sin, but when he does, he will get right out and ask God to forgive him and clean him up, repenting that he got into the mud in the first place. Our nature changes when we truly have a heart change, when we confess to Jesus and ask him to save us. Some day we will be in paradise with God the Father and God the Son and God the Holy Spirit.

LETTER TO THE CHURCH AT SMYRNA

This church age I believe existed from around 96 AD to 316 AD from the time when the last apostle, John died to the coming into power of Constatine, a Christian Caesar over the Roman Empire. This church age suffered great persecution by the Roman Empire. The Roman empire was declining in power with trouble on all their borders and the ruling Caesar blamed the Christians. The Christians were greatly persecuted and were killed for sport in the arenas and feed to lions. These early Christians suffered greatly for the cause of Jesus Christ and cause me to be ashamed of how I serve my Lord today. The historical writer Polycarp listed some of the Christians killed in Smyrna on February 23, 155 AD. Christ finds nothing wrong with this church at Smyrna.

Vs 8   **"And unto the angel of the church in Smyrna write; these things saith the first and the last, which was dead, and is alive;"**

Again Jesus calls himself the first and the last just like verse 8 in Chapter 1, where Jesus calls himself the Alpha and the Omega. John referred to Jesus as being with God in the beginning in John 1:3 and here in Revelations as being in the end. Jesus reminds this church that he was dead but is alive. We worship a living Savior, not one that dead, like all other religions of the world.

Vs 9   **"I know thy works, and tribulation, and poverty, but thou art rich and I**
know the blasphemy of them which say they are Jews, and are not, but are
the synagogue of Satan."

These Christians at Smyrna had works and suffered great tribulation for

their works. I Corinthians 3:11-15 tells us that works are in two categories, gold

silver and precious stones; wood, hay and stubble. Since Jesus finds no fault with

this church, their works were obviously of the gold, silver and precious stone

type. Jesus says that that He knows their poverty. Serving the Lord Jesus Christ

in that day of great persecution meant giving up all their possessions if convicted

of being a Christian. Many of the early Christians gave of their possessions and

food to support the others that were in greater need than themselves. Jesus tells

them they are rich. A Christian's riches are not measured in this worlds

possessions, but in the treasures that are laid up in heaven, like the gold, silver

and precious stone rewards for our works for the Lord Jesus Christ on this earth.

Jesus also knew of the blasphemy of those who say they are Jews and are

not. The term Jews refers to a religious person, one who claims to be religious,

but are of the synagogue of Satan. It is difficult to take the persecution of the

outside forces against the church of Jesus Christ, but when these Christians were

persecuted from within the church by those people that claimed to be religious,

this was the worst kind of persecution that they could have suffered. Jesus calls

these religious persons Satan worshipers, or as John calls them anti-Christ in his

epistles.

Vs 10 **"Fear none of those things which thou shall suffer: behold, the devil shall cast some of you into prison, that ye may be tried; and ye shall have tribulation ten days: be thou faithful unto death, and I will give thee a crown of life."**

Matthew 10:28 **"Fear not them which kill the body, but are not able to kill the soul; but rather fear Him which is able to destroy both the soul and the body in hell."** I John 4:18 **"There is no fear in love; but perfect love casteth out fear; because fear hath torment. he that feareth is not made perfect in love."** A Christian should never fear death, for to be absent from this body is to be present with the Lord Jesus Christ in Heaven. Satan live on fear, and if we do not fear, then we have victory over Satan. These Christians at Smyrna were persecuted for ten years according to "Polycarp" (a historical writer of that day). Jesus will allow us to go through tribulation , but He will only allow us to suffer for a short time and then it will end. Paul tells us in Romans 5:1-4 **"Therefore being justified by faith, we have peace with God through our Lord Jesus Christ: By whom also we have access by faith into this grace wherein we stand, and rejoice in hope of the glory of God. And not only so, but we glory in tribulations also; knowing that tribulation worketh patience; And patience, experience; and experience, hope;"** The more tribulation we endure the more we learn patience, and the more patience we have then will bring more experience. When we see how Jesus has brought us through all the times of tribulation in our lives and worked out our problems, the stronger our hope will

be in trusting in Jesus to deliver us from the times of tribulation in the future.
This is our hope in Jesus Christ. Now if you desire more patience then pray for
more tribulation. We should learn to wait on the Lord to work out tribulations in
our lives, for they will only last for a short time.

There are five crowns spoken of in the Bible. (1) Here the crown of life
will be given to those that are killed for their testimony for the cause of Jesus
Christ, also James 1:12. (2) The incorruptible crown given for the mastery over
the old man (the flesh), I Corinthians 9:25. (3) The crown of rejoicing given to
those who have led others to Jesus Christ, I Thessalonians 2:10. (4) The crown
of righteousness given to those who are looking for the appearing of our Lord
Jesus Christ, 2 Timothy 4:8. (5) The crown of glory for the pastors and
shepherds of the church, 1 Peter 5:4.

Vs 11 **"He that hath an ear, let him hear what the Spirit saith unto the churches;
He that overcometh shall not be hurt of the second death."**

This is a warning to the lost and to the saved to listen to what the Word of
God says and to the wooing of the Holy Spirit leading us to do the biding of Jesus
Christ. He that listens to the Word of God and is saved will overcome the second
death, which is the eternal separation from God in the lake of fire.

LETTER TO THE CHURCH AT PERGAMOS

The Pergamos church age lasted from 316 AD to around 500 AD, with the final fall of the Roman Empire. With Caesar Constantine gaining control of the Roman empire in 316 AD, Christianity was made the state religion. Constantine moved the capital of the Roman empire to Byzantium in 324 AD, where the whole city was rebuilt with marbles and great art objects taken from many of the temples of the Roman gods. During this period of time the temples to the Roman gods were turned into Christian churches. The Roman empire was split into the Western Roman and the Eastern Roman empires. By the year 476 AD the Roman empire was totally overthrown by an invading barbarian army, which brought in the beginning of the dark ages. The Pergamos church age centered around the great city of Rome, which was the seat of the Roman rule over most of the world of that day. Jesus refers to that great city as the seat of Satan in this letter to the church at Pergamos.

Vs 12 **"And to the angle of the church in Pergamos write; These things saith he which hath the sharp sword with two edges:"**

Jesus speaking to this church, warns them with the sharp two-edged sword. Hebrews 4:12 **"For the word of God is quick, and powerful, and sharper than any two-edged sword, piercing even to the dividing asunder of soul and spirit, and of the joints and marrow, and is a discerner of the thoughts and intents of the heart."** The sword speaks of the judgment of the Word of God against this church. When you are living by the word of God, it commends you, but when you are living ins sin, the Word of God judges you. The Word of God cuts both ways; toward the lost it condemns them and points the way of forgiveness toward Jesus Christ, and toward the saved it judges us in sin and reminds us that repentance brings us back into fellowship with our Lord.

Vs 13 **"I know thy works, and where thou dwellest, even where Satan's seat is: and thou holdest fast my name, and hast not denied my faith, even in those days wherein Antipas was my faithful martyr, who was slain among you, where Satan dwelleth."**

Christ Jesus knows their works, and he knows all about our works. This Church dwells where Satan's seat is located. This may refer to beginning of the political movement of the upper class of the church membership ruling over the common membership with the doctrine of the Nicolaitians. Constantine made Christianity the official religion of the Roman empire, which may also refer to the church dwelling where Satan's seat is. We know from history that Pergamos was the very center of idolatry during this time. The Temple to Athena was located in Pergamos, along with a great library. Caesar Agustus and Hadrian built great temples there, and the great temples to Zeus and Bacus was built there. The statue of Bacus, a goat with the head of a man with two horns was located in Pergamos, which many believe is a picture of Satan. A great healing temple and the temple to a serpent god was located there.

Christ commends this church for holding fast the name of Jesus Christ and had not denied their faith. Can you imagine the difficult time Christians had living in this wicked city, with Satan and his demons on every corner seeking to devour them like a roaring lion. These Christians had three things that Jesus commends them for in this verse. 1) They had works, 2) they held fast the name of Jesus Christ and 3) they had not denied their faith in Jesus Christ. Also Christ Jesus commends the martyrdom of Antipus who was slain in the church. Possibly this was the pastor of the church, who stood tall for the cause of Jesus and even gave his life for his testimony. Satan will attack the church at the place he can do the most damage to the testimony of the Christians in the community, and the pastor bears the brunt of the assault most of the time.

Vs 14 **"But I have a few things against thee, because thou hast there them that hold the doctrine of Balaam, who taught Balak to cast a stumbling block before the children of Israel, to eat things sacrificed unto idols, and to commit fornication."**

Jesus also had a few things against this church. This church had a person teaching the people the doctrine of Balak as a doctrine. A doctrine is a truth or principal teaching of the Bible, for the church to follow Jesus Christ in their daily lives. Numbers 25:1-9 tells us the story of Baal-peor, who led the Israelites into worshipping his idols and eating sacrificed meat to these idols. Baal-peor also led the Israelites into committing fornication with his people, the Midianites. Fornication is the sexual activity of the unmarried people of God, and adultery is the sexual activity of the married with other than their spouses. God was so angered that he sent a plague among the Israelites that killed 24,000 men and women. The plague would have continued, but the people repented and began weeping at the tent of the tabernacle. There was a man in the church at Pergamos

teaching the people to commit adultery and fornication as a doctrine of the Bible.

Like Baal-peor this man was teaching that they could serve God by their good

works and still live in sin at the same time. Christ teaches us that we are to

separated from the world and the ways of the world and to be followers of Him

and not followers of Satan. A man cannot serve two masters, he will love one and

hate the other. Jesus tell this church to repent or His judgment will fall on the

people. I Corinthians 10:1-15. Romans 8:5-8. II Peter 2:15. These things are

written in the Bible for an example to us, showing that God will not tolerate

living in unrighteousness like the rest of the world while calling ourselves his

people. Like the judgment on the Israelites in Numbers, Jesus warns this church

to repent of this doctrine of Balak being taught in the church, or judgment will

come on them.

Vs 15 **"So hast thou also them that hold the doctrine of the Nicolatians, which thing
I hate."**

The second thing that Jesus had against this church was those that have

the doctrine of the Nicolaitians. Remember that the church at Ephesus had those

in it that had the deeds of the Nicolaitians, and now this teaching and practice has

become a doctrine being taught in the church. "Nikao" means to conquer or rule

over, and "Laity" means the common people or membership. Hebrews Chapter 8

tells us about our high priest Jesus Christ who mediates at the throne of God in

our behalf day and night. Paul tells us that we no longer need a high priest like

the old testament days where priest after priest ministered at the tabernacle of
God on the earth, and continually brought sacrifices into the altar to offer up to
God year after year. But our High Priest Jesus Christ went into heaven bearing
his own shed blood to be offered upon the altar in heaven once and for all time
for the sins of the entire world, and now is continually ministering to us as we call
upon his name in our time of need on this earth. We no longer need a high priest
on this earth as a go between us and God in heaven. We can put our petitions
before the very throne of God any time of the day and night. Can we do this
through a man on this earth, any time of day or night or any place we are upon
this earth? Of course not. I Timothy 2:5 **"For there is one God, and one
mediator between God and men, the man Christ Jesus."** There is no man on
this earth that is our mediator, in fact Jesus says that he hates this doctrine of the
Nicolaitians.

Vs 16: **"Repent; or else I will come unto thee quickly, and will fight against them
with the sword of my mouth."**

Those that teach these doctrines in the church are warned, to repent, or
else He will come unto them quickly. Like the Israelites in Numbers, God judged
those people who had gone over to Balak's way of worshipping idols and
committing fornication with the people of the Midianites, and they dropped dead
all over the place. Jesus warns that He will fight against them with the sword of
his mouth. Here we have an explanation of the two edged sword that will judge
the world at the end of the tribulation period. The word of Jesus can cut us apart,

separating those things that are wrong from those things that righteous. At the words of Jesus all creation obeys his command, and his word that we have in the Bible is powerful, and will judge us when we are living in sin.

Vs 17: **"He that hath an ear, let him hear what the Spirit saith unto the churches; To him that overcometh will I give him to eat of the hidden manna, and will give him a white stone, and in the stone a new name written, which no man knoweth saving he that receiveth it."**

There are two promises given to them that overcometh Satan and the persecutions in this world for serving Jesus Christ. 1) We shall eat of the hidden manna. In the wilderness, the Israelites were fed six days with bread from heaven, and on the sixth day they gathered enough manna for the Sabbath day also. This manna was the bread of life to the people, it kept them alive and had everything in it that they needed. We will be given this hidden manna, that is not revealed what it is. I believe that this is the bread of eternal life, that we will never hunger again. It is hidden, and I believe if it were revealed, we would not understand anyway. We will eat fruit in heaven from the tree of life as recorded in Revelation 22:2-14. 2) We shall have a white stone given unto us with a new name written on it, that no man will know except you. You and I have a name we received from our fathers all the way back to Adam. Now in heaven we will receive a new name, written on a white stone. The color white symbolizes purity, and our name on this earth was given to a fleshly body that cannot inherit eternal life. In heaven we will have an eternal body give to us by our father in heaven, which will be given a new name. Jesus will give it to us in heaven and only I will

know my new name.

LETTER TO THE CHURCH AT THYATIRA

The Thyatira church age lasted from around 500 AD to about 1500 AD, which is

known as the dark ages or the Medieval Period. The Roman empire was defeated by the

barbarians and was no longer a world power in 476 AD. The formal Roman Church had

gained dominance within the Roman empire and monasteries spread into the neighboring

countries. These monasteries copied the scriptures in Latin. This time period was

dominated by the very wealthy that owned the land with the very poor serving as serfs

under the land owners. The church was taken over by the doctrine of the "Nicolaitians"

with the wealthy being the only ones who knew how to read, becoming the leaders of the

churches. In 800 AD Charlemagne was decreed emperor in Europe and ordered the same

order of formal worship under the Roman Catholic Church throughout Europe. The

worship of mother Mary and baby Jesus was introduced during this time period with the

birth being magnified and not the death of Jesus on the cross, shedding his blood for the

remission of sin. Mass was introduced into the church and the teaching on purgatory

began to be taught during this church age. Around 840 AD the large land owners broke

into small kingdoms, which began the Feudal political system. Walled towns were built

around castles of the wealthy and the poor lived around them for protection against

invading armies. Between 800 to 1300 AD almost all Europe was Christian with the

MOORE ABOUT REVELATION

Pope in Rome as the center of the church. The Pope became a powerful man over almost all the political rulers in Europe. Positions in the church were sold to the wealthy and power struggles between the church and the political leaders of that day were common. Between 1100 and 1270 AD the holy crusades were fought with the Turks over the holy land. The Dark Ages lasted till the time of Martin Luther, who began the Reformation Period in the Roman Catholic church in October, 1517 AD, when he pinned his ninety - five theses to the church doors. This letter to the church at Thyatira is twenty verses long, which is a lengthy letter compared to the others. Christ has a great deal to say about this church.

Vs 18 **"And unto the angel of the church in Thyatiria write; These things saith the Son of God, who hath his eyes like unto a flame of fire, and his feet are like fine brass;"**

Jesus identifies himself as the one who stands in the midst of the candle sticks, which are the angles of the seven churches. Jesus eyes are like unto a flame of fire represent judgment. Like the saved standing before the judgment seat of Jesus Christ, when we will be judged for the works we have done upon this earth, Jesus eyes will look upon our works like a flame of fire. Those works that are like wood, hay and stubble will be burned up under the eyes of Jesus, but the works like gold, silver and precious stones will be tested by the eyes of Jesus and endure the flame of fire. Our works will fall into either of these two categories. The eyes of Jesus will know every work, whether it was from the heart in serving Him or whether from the flesh. Jesus feet are portrayed like fine brass, which also represent judgment. Jesus feet will stamp out unrighteousness and sin in His church.

Vs 19 **"I know thy works, and charity, and service, and faith, and thy patience, and thy works; and the last to be more than the first."**

This church had first works and then latter works, that were even more than the first works. James 2: 17-20 tells us that works are the credentials of faith. That faith without any works shows a dead faith. Works are the life of faith, showing the lost world around us that we really have faith in our Lord Jesus Christ. Even the Devil believes that Jesus is the Son of God, **"but wilt thou know, O vain man, that faith without works is dead?"** This church had "charity" or love. The Pharisees asked Jesus which commandment is the greatest of the Law. Jesus answered them that there are two **"thou shalt love the Lord thy God with all thy heart, mind and soul; and the second commandment is like unto it, thou shalt love thy neighbor as thyself."** Jesus summarized the first five commandments of the Law which deals with mans relationship with God as loving Him with all our heart, mind and soul. Jesus summarized the last five commandments of the Law which deal with mans relationship with man as loving our brother as we love ourselves. This church at Thyatira had love and they had service and faith. Faith is what keeps us serving the Lord Jesus Christ. This church was not just sitting on the pew on Sundays, they were serving Christ. Our faith is seen through our serving Jesus Christ. Jesus knew their patience. Romans 5:3-5 **"We glory in tribulations also; knowing that tribulation**

worketh patience; and patience, experience; and experience, hope." The more

tribulations that we go through, the more we can look back and see what God has

brought us through, to where we stand today. Then tribulations builds our

patience enduring tribulations waiting for God to deliver us, which then builds

our hope. Our hope is not in this world, but in the world to come, we patiently

wait for that day when we will be with the Lord in Heaven. You see then that the

more tribulation that you endure, the more patience you learn and the more hope

you have. This is why the apostles counted it a privilege to have suffered for the

cause of Jesus Christ, for their faith became even stronger in the hope of Christ

return. The people who lived during the Dark Ages suffered a great deal through

plagues, starvation and the tyranny of the wealthy land owners. They had to help

one another and have love for their brother. There are three types of love in the

Greek language used in the original Bible. There is "Eros" or sexual love, there is

"Pheleo" or brotherly love and there is "Agape" or Godly love. "Agape" is the

love that these Christians at Thyatira had. Agape love comes only from God

and is not produced by us. The lost world does not have this Agape love. This is

the love that enables us to love the unlovely, love those that hate us and love that

causes us to want to tell those that we do not even know about Jesus Christ and

what He has done for them on the cross of Calvary.

Vs 20 **"Notwithstanding I have a few things against thee, because thou sufferest**

that woman Jezebel, which calleth herself a prophetess, to teach and seduce

my servants to commit fornication, and to eat things sacrificed unto idols."

Jesus has commended this church and now there are some things that Jesus has against them much like the doctrine of Balaam and the doctrine of the Nicolaitians in the previous church. The leader of the church is called a Jezebel, an adulterous woman. Revelation Chapter 17 refers to a harlot who rides the beast and is explained to be the great city of seven hills, which reigneth over the kings of the earth. This is commonly known as that great city of Rome, which is ruled over by a harlot in the beginning of the tribulation period. This will be explained latter on in this book. Jezebel is a reference back to I Kings Chapter 18-21. This Jezebel in the letter to the church at Thyatira claims to be a prophetess who seduced the people to commit fornication and to eat things sacrificed unto idols. Like the harlot in Revelations Chapter 17, this Jezebel was the leader of the church in this church age. This is what John calls a false prophet in his epistle letters. A false prophet is one who teaches false doctrines claiming authority from the word of God. Why would people follow such teachings? During the Dark Ages the only ones who could read Latin were the church leaders, and the people were being told what the Word of God said. The Bible was translated only into Latin by the Monks in this time period and it was not until Martin Luther translated the Bible into German, that the common man was able to read the bible for himself. I Kings records that Jezebel was married to King Ahab, and she worshipped idols and kept and fed 400 prophets to Bail. She was in open rebellion to the nation of Israel and the worship of Jehovah God. This Jezebel in the church at Thyatira taught spiritual fornication against the

Word of God. The church is referred to as the bride of Christ, and when the church serves Satan and lives in sin all week long and then comes back to her husband Jesus Christ on Sunday to ask forgiveness, then this is spiritual fornication. The people were being taught that they could live in sin and as long as they came to church to ask forgiveness or take communion, then they were forgiven.

During the Dark Ages in 590 AD Gregory I became the first Pope of the Roman Catholic Church. All of Europe was dominated by the leadership of the church at Rome during this period of the church age till the Reformation period under the leadership of Martin Luther, who began the Protestant movement.

Vs 21 **"And I gave her space to repent of her fornication; and she repented not."**

Christ will not condemn us without first letting us know where we have gone wrong, and give us space to repent. If we are wrong in our doctrine, we will be shown the error in which we teach or live. I believe Martin Luther was such a man that God used to reveal to the church of that day, the corruption and error of doctrine being taught to the people. The Protestant movement spread all over Europe during the following church age.

Vs 22 **"Behold, I will cast her into bed, and them that commit adultery with her into great tribulation, except they repent of their deeds."**

If people will not repent of known sin, and here it is the sin of spiritual fornication under the leadership of Jezebel, then God will make it convenient for them to commit such a sin, and there is no better place to do so than in a bed

together. Those people that follow her will be cast into bed with her so all can

see just where they stand in their believing her prophesies. This bed was not for

enjoyment in their sin, but for great tribulation. During the Dark Ages all of

Europe suffered the great plague, where millions of people died.

Vs 23 **"And I will kill her children with death; and all the churches shall know that**
I am he which searcheth the reigns and hearts; and I will give unto every one
of you according to your works."

Except they repent of their deeds, Jesus will kill Jezebel's children with

death. This may refer to physical death or spiritual death in hell or both. The

people that will not repent will receive their just reward. Jesus knows their works

and the intent of the heart in every thing that we do. This is proof of our being

saved, when we sin, the Holy Spirit will convict us of that sin and continually

urge us to repent and get out of sin. If we persist in living in sin there will come

a point in time when Jesus will not tolerate our rebellion against the Holy Spirit,

and Jesus will take our life prematurely. If we are causing problems in the church

and we refuse to repent, then we had better be ready to die. Paul said that if we

cause one little one to stumble and fall by our example in the church, then it were

better for us that a mill stone be hung around our neck and cast into the sea to

drown.

Vs 24 **"But unto you I say, and unto the rest in Thyatira, as many as have not this doctrine, and which have not known the depth of Satan, as they speak; I will put upon you none other burden."**

Not everyone followed this Jezebel and her doctrine which came from Satan himself. All false doctrines that teach contrary to the word of God, come from the lips of Satan himself. Jesus knows these true believers hardships and burdens and promises not to put any more burdens than what they have endured already.

Vs 25 **"But that which ye have already hold fast till I come."**

Just hold onto the faith that you have till I come. What a statement for the church today with all the false doctrines being taught across all the churches in the world today. What is our faith based on? **"Faith cometh by hearing and hearing by the Word of God."** How do we grow in faith? If the man we are listening to is teaching something that is not taught by the Word of God, then we better listen to the Word of God. The more of the Word of God that we learn, the more our faith will be in it. Who are the ones that are so easily led astray by the false teachers? Those people that are new converts and the people that just attend church and have no desire to read the word of God for themselves will be easily led astray with every wind of doctrine that comes along. When we study the Word of God and desire to know what it says, then the Holy Spirit will give us understanding and we will know when something does not agree with the Bible.

Vs 26 **"And he that overcometh, and keepeth my works unto the end, to him will I give power over the nations."**

Christ will not allow any more burdens and temptations placed on us than we are able to bear. When the church is going through tribulations and trials, the faithful who are still doing the work of witnessing, serving and striving for the cause of Christ, God will not place any more burdens on us. If you do not want any more burdens placed on you, then become more active in the work of Jesus in the church. Jesus knows our works. A promise of Jesus to those who hold onto their faith will be given power over the nations. Later on we will talk about the church ruling and reigning over the nations of this earth during the thousand year reign. I Corinthians 6:**2 "Do ye not know that the saints shall judge the world."**

Vs 27 **"And he shall rule them with a rod of iron; as the vessels of a potter shall they be broken to shivers; as I received of my Father."**

This is a direct reference to the saints ruling and reigning over the remnant during the thousand year reign on this earth with Christ Jesus. As Jesus receives this promise from the Father, He promises that we will share this promise with him.

Vs 28 **"And I will give him the morning star."**

Chapter 22:16 Jesus identifies himself as the bright morning star. As Jesus rose from the grave on Easter morning as the bright morning star, the first fruits of the resurrection, He promises to those who believe in Him that they also shall rise like the bright morning star (Jesus) to meet him in the air in the resurrection.

Vs 29 **"He that hath an ear, let him hear what the Spirit saith unto the churches."**

Notice that this warning to listen to the Spirit is to all the churches and not just to the church at Thyatira. Those that are living in sin and following after this Jezebel must repent quickly and listen to the urging of the Holy Spirit or this judgment of Jesus Christ will fall on them.

REVELATION CHAPTER 3

LETTER TO THE CHURCH AT SARDIS

The Sardis church age I believe lasted from 1,500 AD to around 1,800 AD which is referred to as the Reformation age. The largest cities all over Europe began to build large churches, competing with each other trying to build the largest and tallest church. Architecture had developed the design of large open domed areas of worship with barrel vaulted crossing chambers to form a cross shaped building. As the buildings became taller and taller in competing with the cities around them, the churches began to take on an appeal of being close to heaven with the large domed center sanctuary, which was painted with frescos by well known artist. Porticos were set in the side aisles with statues of the saints which the people often came to pray to. During this church age the mother and the child statues became the dominant figure in the church, which the people were taught to pray to the mother of Jesus for intercession for them in heaven. Almost all of these churches today no longer have worship services in them. During this church age the Roman Catholic Church was involved in political maters and had great power in the world of that day. A power struggle began between the church and the rulers of the developing countries in Europe. The Roman Catholic Church had become corrupt in selling positions in the church to the wealthy and had control of almost all Europe. Kings began to depart from the commands made by the church and excommunication's from the church were frequently used to keep them in control. Martin Luther began to speak out against the corruption in the church at Rome and pinned his ninety-five theses to the church doors in October, 1517 AD. Martin Luther translated the Bible from Latin to German, which gave the people the chance to read the Bible for themselves for the first time. The printing press was also invented at this same time, which predominantly reproduced literature on the Bible at first. The Protestant movement grew and the people began to turn away from the Roman Catholic Church. The Church at England split away from the control by Rome and the Pope, which slowly took the power of the Roman Catholic Church away from the kings and political leaders in Europe. The letter to the church at Sardis is speaking directly to the corruption in the church of this period. Jesus speaking unto the church at Sardis has nothing good to say about this church.

Vs 1　**"And unto the angel of the church in Sardis write; These things saith he that hath the seven Spirits of God, and the seven stars; I know thy works, that thou hast a name that thou livest, and art dead."**

The name "Sardis" means "those who came out of." Their name may refer to those who survived the Dark Ages with thousands of people dying from starvation and disease in that time period. Their name may also refer to the reformation period when the Protestant movement came out of the Roman Catholic Church. This church age had great works in building and the people donated materials and time in the building of these great church buildings. Jesus says that they had a name among all of Europe that they were alive, but they were dead.

Vs 2   **"Be watchful, and strengthen the things which remain, that are ready to die: for I have not found thy works perfect before God."**

Why were the things which remain ready to die? They were not watching that the works they were doing were not found perfect before God. God was not pleased with this church. I believe that the ones who knew the word of God, the leaders in the church were not watching and keeping the church focused on Jesus Christ and winning the lost around them, and they lost their strength.

Vs 3   **"Remember therefore how thou hast received and heard, and hold fast, and repent. If therefore thou shalt not watch, I will come on thee as a thief, and thou shalt not know what hour I will come upon thee."**

Jesus tells them what to watch for. Remember how you were saved and received the word of God. **"Salvation cometh by faith, and faith by hearing the Word of God."** When we first were saved remember the fire that burned inside of us and we wanted to serve the Lord Jesus and now the fire is not as hot as it once was. Repent and watch or Jesus will come as a thief in the night and remove the candlestick from its place like the warning to the church at Ephesus. It is true that almost all the great churches built in the 1500 AD to 1800 AD period are just buildings of great architecture today, and no worship is held in

them. When sin creeps into our lives, we gradually lose sight of where we are
going till we finally just quit serving Jesus Christ. Psalms 1: 1 **"Blessed is the
man that walketh not in the council of the ungodly, nor standeth in the way of
sinners, nor siteth in the seat of the scornful."** Notice the progression of losing
God's blessing in our lives. We begin to walk with the ungodly, then we stand in
the way of sinners, to the point that we sit down with the scornful.

Vs 4 **"Thou hast a few names even in Sardis which have not defiled their
garments; and they shall walk with me in white: for they are worthy."**

When the vast majority have fallen by the wayside and follow after
worldly power seeking leaders, then the few that still walk with the Lord Jesus are
called worthy to walk in white with the Lord. God has always had a remnant that
still served him. Romans 11:1-5 tells us how God will always have a remnant,
even today. God wants to use us today in his church and if we will not be his
servants, then he will use someone else and we will miss the blessings that God
wants to give to us. Like our natural fathers, when we fall into sin God will have
to chasten us as his children. He has to whip us, so to speak, till we repent and
serve him as we should. Our natural fathers gave us ice cream when we were
good, but when we were bad, our fathers could not give us good things, but had to
chasten us. God is the same way, when we are serving him we receive his
blessings. Now if we do not receive the chastening of God when we fall into sin,

then we are not his children, but are bastards as the scripture says. Our natural fathers did not go over to the neighbors children and whip them when they were being bad. They were not his children. God only chastens his own children also. If we are living in sin and God does not chasten us, then we are Satan's children and Satan does not care about us like God does. Revelations 3:19 **"As many as I love, I rebuke and chasten: be zealous therefore, and repent."**

Vs 5   **"He that overcometh, the same shall be clothed in white raiment; and I will not blot out his name out of the book of life, but I will confess his name before my Father, and before his angels."**

White is a symbol of purity and of the grace of God making us pure by the blood of Jesus Christ. This robe of righteousness that is given to all who trust in Jesus as their Lord and Savior covers our unrighteousness and when God looks upon us, all He sees is the blood of Jesus as a pure white robe without spot. Their names will not be blotted out of the book of life. Revelations 13:8 and 22:19 tells us about those who do not have their names written in the Lambs book of life will be left on the Earth to go through the terrible judgments of God upon this Earth. Not only must we accept Jesus as our Lord and Savior, but we must confess that the Bible is true and is God' Word. All those men through time that have tried to destroy the Bible, like Adolph Hitler, and have tried to prove the Bible was not God's inspired Word, will also have their names removed from the book of life.

I understand that every person that will ever be born on this Earth has their name written in the book of life and when that person reaches the age of accountability, and have not professed Jesus Christ as their Lord and Savior will have their name blotted out of the book of life. The marvelous thing is that when a person does accept Jesus Christ as their savior, dying on the cross of Calvary shedding his blood for their sins, then their name is rewritten into the book of life. Jesus tells us that He will confess our name before the Father and his angels in heaven.

Vs 6   **"He that hath an ear, let him hear what the Spirit saith unto the churches."**

The conclusion to this church at Sardis is that they hear the Word of God and repent of their sins.

LETTER TO CHURCH AT PHILADELPHIA

This letter to the church at Philadelphia represents the church age from around 1800 AD to the present day. We are living in this church age and is written specifically to us as Christians today. This age in which we are living is referred to as the Reformation Period and the Industrialization period. Martin Luther pinned his ninety-five thesis to the Roman Catholic Church doors in October, 1517 AD which ultimately brought about the reformation period and the Protestant movement. The Bible was translated into German and into English and the printing press helped spread the news of

Jesus Christ and salvation by His shed blood on the cross of Calvary and by faith in Jesus

as savior. The Roman Catholic Church had restricted the interpretation of the Bible to

only the priest from the Latin Bible and the doctrine of salvation by the power of the

Pope to save or excommunicate men and women from heaven. Martin Luther began

preaching that the Bible teaches salvation comes only through faith in Jesus Christ.

The letter to this church is only the second that finds no fault with the church.

This church age will last till verse 10 and eleven are fulfilled. The rapture of the Church

is promised to the true church but the apostate church will be left to go through the

tribulation period under the letter to the church at Laodicea. As discussed earlier the

church (all the people who have trusted in Jesus Christ as their Lord and Savior) will be

raptured out of this world as we know it, when Jesus comes in the air. There are two

stages of Jesus coming again back to this earth. I Thessalonians 4:13-18 tells us that

Jesus will come back in a cloud just like He left this earth. The dead shall rise from their

graves first with a new body just like the body of Jesus and their soul and spirit which

was in heaven with Jesus will be placed in their new body. Then those who are alive will

be changed with a new body just like Jesus with their soul and spirit in this new body.

All those that have believed Jesus died for their sins and that Jesus rose from the grave

just like the Bible says that he did, will be caught up in the air to go to heaven with Jesus.

All this will happen in the twinkling of an eye just like I Corinthians 15:52 records. The

second coming of Jesus to this earth as King of kings and Lord of lord to rule on this

earth for a thousand years will be covered in Revelations chapter 19. Jesus coming in the air is at the beginning of the tribulation period and at the end of the Philadelphia church age. Jesus coming back to this earth is at the end of the tribulation period of forty-two months or seven years after His coming in the air.

Vs 7   **"And to the angel of the church in Philadelphia write; These things saith he that is holy, he that is true, he that hath the key of David, he that openeth, and no man shutteth; and shutteth, and no man openeth."**

Jesus addresses himself four ways:

1) He that is holy. Christ is the only one that can say this. He is the only one who has righteousness and holiness is no imputed on him. We have righteousness but it is imputed on us by what Jesus did on the cross. God's holy law is totally satisfied by the blood of Jesus Christ which was shed for us.

2) He that is true. Christ was true to God's will for his life by giving up paradise with God to come to this earth to suffer and to die for us. Christ was true to man for living up to his promise to all the Old Testament saints who trusted in him to deliver them from their sins, and to those who followed Jesus while on this earth. The significance of what Jesus did for us could be compared to us as a human being going down to become an ant, giving up all the things we love and enjoy in order to suffer all the things an ant suffers and to give up our life to die for all the ants so that they could be saved. What Jesus did for us does not even compare to that, but you may see what a great sacrifice Jesus made for us to come to this

earth, giving up all his glory in heaven to take on mortal flesh and to suffer as he did for us.

3) He that hath the keys of David. This is a reference to Isaiah 22:22 where Eliakim the steward of Hezekiah held the keys to the palace in Jerusalem. Jesus is referring to himself as the Key providing access to God for us.

4) He that openeth and no man shutteth, and shutteth and no man openeth. If God be for us then the Word of God says who can be against us. When God opens doors for us then no man can shut that door, and when God shuts a door no man can open that door. I believe this reference may follow what Jesus said in Revelations 1:18 "I am he that liveth, and was dead; and behold, I am alive for evermore. A-men; and have the keys of hell and of death." When Jesus says that there is an open door set before us in the next verse, there is no man on this earth that can shut that door and tell us that we have been excommunicated from God. Jesus has the keys to hell and to death, and as far as that goes the keys to heaven as well. In Acts chapter 2 on the day of Pentecost when the Holy Spirit came to this earth to dwell among men, the keys of heaven were given to Peter to open up salvation through the preached Word of God and faith in Jesus Christ where 3,000 Jews believe that Jesus died and rose again for their sins. The kingdom of Heaven was opened to the Jews that day. In Acts chapter 10 Peter again was given the keys of Heaven to open the door of salvation to the gentile. The house of Corneillus being the first gentiles to saved by their faith in Jesus Christ. The

keys to heaven are not mentioned again till here in Revelations where Jesus has the keys. Jesus is going to shut that door of salvation during the tribulation and no man will be able to open that door.

The kingdom of Heaven is still open today. Acts 14:27 the door was opened to the gentiles for salvation. I Corinthians 16:9 and II Corinthians 2:12 tells us that the door is open. John 10:1-11 tells us that Jesus is the door of salvation and no man comes to God but through him.

Vs 8 **"I know thy works: behold, I have set before thee an open door, and no man can shut it; for thou hast a little strength, and hast kept my word, and hast not denied my name."**

Today a man opens the door for most churches and a man can shut that door. But when Jesus opens that door for us to serve him in his church, then no man can shut that door. The churches that have kept his Word and not denied that Jesus is the Christ as the savior of this world, then have an open door to his work and no man can shut that door. Many people are still being saved through the preaching of God's Word throughout the world today. This door is still open Revelations 22:17-19.

Vs 9 **"Behold, I will make them of the synagogue of Satan, which say they are Jews, and are not, but do lie; behold, I will make them to come and worship before thy feet, and to know that I have loved thee."**

Jews here in this verse are not those nationally, but those spiritually that think and teach like the Jews in their attitude. They think that their way of religion is the only way to come to God and that a man opens the door to heaven for them. This is the great difference between the Protestant and Catholic religion today. The philosophy like the Jews having the only way to get to heaven is a lie, Jesus says. Jesus tells us that this apostate church is the synagogue of Satan and that they will ultimately some day worship at our feet as we stand with Jesus at his great white throne judgment and know that Jesus has loved us and not them. All the lost will bow their knee to Jesus then and worship him, but it will be to late then, for judgment will be passed on them for their non belief and be cast into hell with the false prophet and the false Christ and Satan to be punished forever and ever (Revelations 20:11-15).

Vs 10 **"Because thou hast kept the word of my patience, I also will keep thee from the hour of temptation, which shall come upon all the world, to try them that dwell upon the earth."**

This is a wonderful promise to the true church that it will not go into the tribulation period. The true church or all true believers in Jesus as their Lord and Savior have kept the word of Jesus patience like Paul records in II Thessalonians chapter one. The true believers have faith and patience while suffering the persecutions and tribulations of this life not only from Satan but the apostate church. During the Reformation age the Protestant churches suffered much persecution and anyone who supported them was excommunicated from the Roman Catholic church. The true church demonstrates their patience waiting for the return of Jesus, looking for him to come back like Paul describes in Romans 8:15-24 **"For we are saved by hope: but hope that is seen is not hope: for what a man seeth, why doth he yet hope for?"** Hebrews 11:6 **"But without faith it is impossible to please him; for he that cometh to God must believe that he is, and that he is a rewarder of them that diligently seek him."** II Corinthians 5:7 **"For we walk by faith, not by sight"**

God's judgment will fall upon all the world, to try them that dwell upon this earth. The true church during this Philadelphia church age will not go through the tribulation period as Jesus promises here in this verse. As recorded in Genesis 7:1-16, Noah and his family were the only righteous people on the earth and God destroyed the earth with a flood. Not one drop of water fell before the Ark was finished and all the inhabitants were safely sealed inside the boat. The righteous did not suffer the judgment of God. **"As it were in the days of Noah,** so shall it be in the days of the coming of the Son of Man." Lot, his wife and daughters were ushered by two angels out of those wicked cities Sodom and Gomorra before God's judgment of fire and brimstone rained down on those cities. **"As it were in the days of Sodom and Gomora so shall it be in the days of the coming of the Son of Man."** God's righteous will not go through the tribulation period of seven years on this earth.

Vs 11 **"Behold, I come quickly: hold that fast which thou hast, that no man take thy crown."**

Jesus speaking to the Philadelphia church age, tells us that he is coming quickly. The Bible says that Jesus is coming in the twinkling of an eye. There will not be time to for the procrastinator to make up his mind to accept Jesus as his Lord and Savior. Hold fast that faith that you have, so that no man will be able to take your crown. Notice that Jesus says take away their rewards, not their salvation.

There is an order of events left to come- II Thessalonians 2:1-12

1.) Vs 1 The rapture of the saints of God by Jesus coming in the air.

2.) Vs 3 After the rapture there will be a falling away of the teaching of Jesus Christ and the Bible by the apostate church left on this earth and the revealing of the son of perdition or the anti-Christ.

3.) Vs 4 The anti-Christ will exhalt himself as god to be worshipped by the whole world. He sits on a throne in the holy of holies in the temple at Jerusalem.

4.) Vs 6-7 The removal of the Holy Spirit which restrains the lawless one from taking control of this world until the true church is removed from this earth. This is called the mystery of iniquity.

5.) Vs 8-10 The revealing of the lawless one with all the power of Satan.

6.) Vs 8 The second coming of Jesus who destroys the anti-Christ with the spirit of his mouth and the brightness of his coming.

7.) Vs 12 The day of judgment of all the wicked who follow the anti-Christ.

Vs 12 **"Him that overcometh will I make a pillar in the temple of my God, and he shall go no more out; and I will write upon him the name of my God, and the name of the new city of my God, which is new Jerusalem, which cometh down out of heaven from my God: and I will write upon him my new name."**

During this Philadelphia church age, those who overcome the power of Satan and his temptations and have faith in Jesus Christ will be made pillars in the temple of God in heaven. The true church shall dwell in the temple of God and will live in the new Jerusalem in the new heaven and earth created after the end of the thousand year reign of Jesus on this present earth. The pillars represent the main supports, something unmovable and anchored to the foundation which is

Jesus Christ. Jesus will write upon the true believers the name of God and the name of the new Jerusalem and they will be given a new name. Much like the marriage of a man and a woman, Jesus will come for his bride (the true church) and carry her to his home in heaven and gives to her a new home and a new name and Jesus will dwell with his bride forever. This is a wonderful promise to this Philadelphia church age.

Vs 13 **"He that hath an ear, let him hear what the Spirit saith unto the churches."**

We are to hear these warnings to the churches and hold onto our faith and not listen to the false teachers of the apostate church.

LETTER TO THE CHURCH AT LAODICEA

This letter is to the apostate church that is left on the earth after the rapture of the true church in the Philadelphia church age. This church will only last for the first forty-two months of the tribulation period. This is the final church age and the church will not be mentioned again. From this point on in Revelation the true church will be referred to as the bride and the apostate church will be referred to as the great harlot. A harlot is a strong word to use in referring to this church, but it portrays the picture of a woman that has a husband in name only and is in love with another man. She is the apostate church.

The anti-Christ will use this church to be worshipped by the whole world as god. I believe that the anti-Christ will use this church to find the lost or stored arch of the covenant and the ashes of the red heifer to give to Israel to restore the ancient temple worship with sacrifices unto God like they did before Israel was destroyed as a nation by Titus in 70 AD. The nation of Israel will accept this anti-Christ as the messiah they are looking for and will worship him also, like the rest of the world. The Jews will worship the anti-Christ until the middle of the seven years of the tribulation when he sits in the holy of holies in the temple to be worshipped by the world as god. We will cover this later on in the book of Revelations.

Note in this letter to the church at Laodicea:

1.) Note Jesus message to this church.

2.) Note the condition of this church.

3.) Note counsel Jesus gives this church.

4.) Note Jesus is knocking at the door and has been shut out of this church.

5.) Note the promise to this church.

Vs 14 **"And unto the angel of the church of the Laodicean's write; These things saith the A-men, the faithful and true witness, the beginning of the creation of God."**

Jesus wants this church to know who is speaking to them. 1.) Jesus is the A-men. Literally God the A-men. God called himself the beginning and the end, the alpha and the omega. Here Jesus calls himself God the end or the end of the church age. 2.) Jesus the faithful and true witness. Jesus has been faithful to his Word and he was a witness on this earth of God's love for us, even to giving up his life for us on the cross of Calvary. 3.) Jesus is the beginning of the creation of God. John 1:1 states this to us. Jesus was in the beginning with God in the creation. This is a direct assault against the Darwin theory that is being taught today as a fact. Man's evolution into what he is today is Satan's lie that is being taught as speculation today, and the revelation of God's Word that man was created along with all the creation will no longer be taught in this church age. Jesus is reminding them that he was in the beginning when God created man. You must believe in speculation or revelation.

Vs 15 **"I know thy works, that thou art neither cold or hot; I would thou were cold or hot."**

Vs 16 **"So then because thou art lukewarm, and neither cold or hot, I will spew thee out of my mouth."**

Jesus said this to all the previous six churches as a commendation, but here this is a condemnation to them. Their works are like water that is lukewarm and makes him sick to his stomach and spews them out of his mouth. This church has the name of being Christian, but in reality they were like the church at Sardis, they were dead. Jesus can work with a cold church and they can be saved or he can work with a hot church to encourage them on, but a church that thinks they are saved and do not need anything, Jesus cannot deal with them at all.

Vs 17 **"Because thou sayest, I am rich, and increased with goods, and have need of nothing; and knowest not that thou art wretched, and miserable, and poor, and blind, and naked:"**

Jesus has nothing good to say about this church. Have you ever heard a church member say that they did not owe anything, and had a bank account that would take care of them in the future? That church fits into this church's category. God does not need a savings account, he needs us to get the gospel out to the world and that cost money. 1.) Jesus says that they are wretched, or deeply afflicted or mortally wounded. They were not able to carry out God's will and function as a church in winning the lost to believe in Jesus as their Lord and Savior. 2.) Jesus says that they were miserable or uncomfortable even with all their riches they could not find happiness. The times in my life that I quit serving the Lord Jesus in his church and just sat on the pew letting others carry out the work of getting the gospel message out to the lost, was the most miserable times of my life. When we loose the joy of our salvation, it is miserable. The times that I was working hard and serving the Lord in every spare minute that I could find were the happiest days of my life. 3.) Jesus says that they were poor. Even the wealthy can loose their wealth. Many a man has lost everything he had and very quickly compared to how long it took him to get his riches. The bible tells us to lay our treasures up in heaven and not on this earth. The riches in heaven can not be moth eaten or rust, but last for eternity. This church thought they were rich, but in heaven they were stone broke, they had no gold, silver and precious stone rewards. 4.) Jesus says that they were blind. They were totally unaware of their condition. They could not see how destitute they really were. They had totally closed their eyes to the truth of God's Word. 5.) Jesus says that they were naked. They had no covering at all, speaking of the blood and forgiveness of sin. We have a robe of righteousness in heaven with the blood of Jesus which covers us and God can only see the blood of his son when he looks upon us. Our sins cannot be seen at all or even remembered with the blood of Jesus covering them.

Vs 18 **"I counsel thee to buy of me gold tried in the fire, that thou mayest be clothed, and that the shame of thy nakedness do not appear; and anoint thine eyes with eyesalve, that thou mayest see."**

Jesus counsels them to do these things. They needed to have gold or rewards laid up in heaven. They needed to have a covering in order to get into heaven and that covering is the blood of Jesus Christ. White raiment is the

picture of the righteousness that is imputed upon us by the blood of Jesus through

our faith in him as the Son of God. Laodicea was known for a clay in this area

that was made into an eyesalve, sold all over the world in that day. Later analysis

of this clay revealed that this clay had no medical property for healing at all.

Jesus tells them that they needed to buy eyesalve to anoint their eyes that would

really open their eyes spiritually as to their condition of being lost.

Vs 19 **"As many as I love, I rebuke and chasten: be zealous therefore, and repent."**

In nature you pull off the suckers on corn and tomatoes so that the fruit

gets bigger and better. You prune the grape vine so that the fruit is fuller and

tastier. God does the same things to us as his children. He chastens us when we

are living in sin and rebukes us by his Word. The Holy Spirit convicts us when

we are wrong and wants us to get back on the straight and narrow road in life.

God does not chasten Satan's children, but his own. Like our fathers, we want to

reward our children for doing right and give good things to them, how much more

does our heavenly father want to reward us for serving him. God cannot reward

us and give us good things while we are living in sin, so we miss God's blessings

when are living in sin. Be zealous or get hot or get on fire, or get saved and

repent therefore, if you do not have the chastening and rebuking of God in your

life.

Vs 20 **"Behold, I stand at the door, and knock: if any man hear my voice, and opens the door, I will come in to him, and I will sup with him, and he with me."**

Jesus has been locked out of this church. They have rejected Jesus, but Jesus has not rejected them. Jesus wants them to repent and accept him. Jesus is knocking on the door, but they have not heard him. The invitation, I believe, will be open for the people to be saved till the middle of the tribulation period when all the people of the world will wear the mark of the beast or the have the seal of God in their forehead. Then and only then, will a persons destination for heaven or hell be determined and the Holy Spirit will no longer be on this earth. Then the wrath of God will be poured out onto this world in the last forty-two months of the tribulation period.

Vs 21 **"To him that overcometh will I grant to sit with me in my throne, even as I also overcame, and am set down with my Father in his throne."**

This is a picture of the great white throne judgment, where the lost will be judged and those saved during the church ages will sit with Jesus in the great white throne. To him that overcometh during this church age and accepts Jesus Christ as their Lord and Savior will suffer greatly for their commitment to Jesus. We are told in chapter thirteen that those people who will be saved during the tribulation will give their lives as their testimony for Jesus. All those who do not

bow down and worship the anti-Christ and still confess Jesus Christ will have

their heads chopped off. Jesus was persecuted and eventually gave his life for his

testimony as being God's son. Jesus makes a promise to those who will accept

him during this Laodicean church age, that they will sit with him in judgment

over those who take their lives.

Vs 22 **"He that hath an ear, let him hear what the spirit saith unto the churches."**

REVELATION CHAPTER 4

In chapter four John is on the Isle of Patmos where he has heard Jesus tell him to write letters to the seven churches in Asia Minor. Chapter four open and the scene changes from the earth to heaven and continues in heaven till chapter 22:5. Many believe that John was physically taken to heaven and some believe he was just in a trance. I believe that John was carried in time to the actual rapture of the church where he was caught up with all the other believers in Jesus Christ, and witnessed first hand the events that he saw. John was not asleep, for in chapter one, verse two, John says he saw these things. Jesus told John in chapter one, verse nineteen, to write the things that he has seen, the things which are and the things which shall be hereafter. John was obviously writing all these things down as he saw them. Jesus even tells John to shut his book in chapter ten and verse four, and do not write what the seven thunders uttered. What John did write, he put into the only words he knew about to describe what he saw. I can imagine that the things he saw a first century man, brought forward into the twentieth century to see for the first time, made it difficult to write and describe what he actually saw. This generation can better understand the descriptions of what John saw than any generation before. I believe this book is written to the Philadelphian church age to give us warning that these things are coming quickly.

Vs 1   **"After this I looked, and behold, a door was opened in heaven: and the first voice which I heard was as it were of a trumpet talking with me; which said, Come up hither, and I will show thee things which must be hereafter."**

A door in heaven opens and a voice like a trumpet is talking to John. This is a picture of the rapture as Paul records in I Corinthians 15:52 and in I Thessalonians 4:16-17 **"For the Lord himself shall descend from heaven with a shout, with the voice of the archangel, and with the trump of God: and the dead in Christ shall rise first: Then we which are alive and remain shall be caught up together with them in the clouds, to meet the Lord in the air: and so shall we ever be with the Lord."** The true church is called the bride of Christ and Jesus is coming for his bride. The parable of the ten virgins at the marriage feast were looking for the bridegroom to come in Matthew 25:1-13. It was customary in that day for the bridegroom to come for his bride at a late hour to try to catch the party by surprise. There were ten virgins that took their lamps to go out to meet the bridegroom when he came. Five of them were wise and took extra oil for their lamps and five were foolish and took just their lamps and no oil at all. At midnight the call came that the bridegroom was coming and the five virgins that had no oil tried to get the others to give them of their oil, but they refused lest there not be enough for them. While the foolish virgins went out to buy oil, the bridegroom came and they went into the marriage and the door was shut. The foolish virgins came and knocked on the door and the Lord told them I know you not and opened not the door. This parable teaches us about the rapture, in that there will be a true church and there will be an apostate church. The true church has oil in their lamps, which represents the Holy Spirit. The apostate church has no oil in their lamps and while they may hear that the Lord or

bridegroom is coming, they will not see him when he comes. The apostate

church will be left out and the door locked.

Vs 2   **"And immediately I was in the spirit: and, behold, a throne was set in**

heaven, and one sat on the throne."

In the twinkling of an eye, could have been written here. The very first

thing that John sees is a throne and one sat on the throne. We serve a living God

and He is reigning over this world today, waiting for the exact time to come for

his bride.

Vs 3   **"And he that sat was to look upon like a jasper and a sardine stone: and**

there was a rainbow round about the throne, in sight like unto an emerald."

John describes the one that sat on the throne. John compares him to a

sardine and a jasper stone. The breastplate of the high priest in the temple in

Jerusalem had twelve stones in it. The sardine was the first stone and the last was

a jasper stone described in Exodus 28:17-20. The first and the last stone, the

alpha and the omega. The one who sits on the throne is the first and last, the God

of Abraham, God our father. A rainbow is a picture of the covenant that God

made with man that he would not destroy the earth again by a flood. This rainbow is a picture of his promises all through his word to those that trust in Jesus as their Lord and Savior.

Vs 4 **"And round about the throne were four and twenty seats: and upon the seats I saw four and twenty elders sitting, clothed in white raiment; and they had on their heads crowns of gold."**

White raiment identifies them as being washed by the blood of the Lamb of God, or saved persons. I believe these may represent the twelve tribes of the seed of Abraham and the twelve apostles of Jesus Christ. These may represent all those that were saved during the Old Testament time and all those that were saved during the New Testament time. Their crowns represent their rewards for how they have served God and their faith while on this earth.

There are five crowns mentioned in the Bible that we will be rewarded with:

1.) Ministers crown

2.) Soul winners crown

3.) Crowns of righteousness

4.) Crown of life

5.) Crown of rejoicing

This may be where those gold, silver and precious stone rewards are placed on our heads in heaven for our rewards.

Vs 5 **"And out of the throne proceeded lightning's and thundering and voices: and there were seven lamps of fire burning before the throne, which are the seven Spirits of God."**

In the old testament the holy of holies had a lampstand with seven oil filled holders that burned day and night, referred to Exodus 37:23. The lampstand represented the Holy Spirit. Now if the Holy Spirit has seven parts, I do not know. We are just told there is seven parts to the Holy Spirit. Lightning and thundering represents the power of the words of God. Jesus words are all powerful and all things obey his words. There is power even in the Bible, when we quote the Word of God, all creation and even the Devil and his demons must obey the words of Jesus. The Word of God has the power to save our souls, by what he promises to us who trust in it. A person cannot deny the Bible and be saved, for what a man denies is what has the power to save him. These lightening and thunders may be a preview of the judgment of God on those who are left on the earth below.

Vs 6 **"And before the throne there was a sea of glass like unto crystal: and in the midst of the throne, and round about the throne, were four beast full of eyes before and behind."**

There is a sea around the throne that looks like crystal glass. John latter describes the streets of heaven in Revelation 21:18 **"And the building of the wall of it was of jasper: and the city was pure gold, like unto clear glass."** I understand that if gold could be refined to pure gold it would be like clear glass, and this is just what John is describing here. Again the Bible must be divinely inspired, for man did not know this till the twentieth century. In the Old Testament there stood a brass vessel which was filled with water in which the ashes of the red heifer were sprinkled for the high priest to wash before he entered the holy of holies to offer up the sacrifices on the mercy seat of the arch of the covenant. This vessel was called the sea. The priest had to be cleansed by the sacrifice of the red heifer which was taken out of the gate of the temple and burned with certain types of wood, representing the sacrifice of Jesus. Before the high priest could enter the holy of holies he had to have the cleansing by the sacrificed ashes in this sea. The only things that can enter into heaven must be pure. This sea of pure gold that John saw may represent the blood of Jesus Christ that was shed on the cross of Calvary, and no one can approach the throne without the blood of Jesus. What a beautiful sight this must have been for John. Now John describes the four beast full of eyes around the throne.

Vs 7   **"And the first beast was like a lion, and the second beast like a calf, and the third beast had a face as a man, and the fourth beast was like a flying eagle."**

The actual interpretation of beast is "four living creatures." These living creatures may be the same creatures that Ezekiel saw at the river Chebar in Ezekiel 1:4-28. Ezekiel describes them in detail, and they sound like the same description as what John sees. These four living creatures surround the Lord in Ezekiel's vision much like what John sees around the throne in heaven. These creatures also could be like the cherubim that were put around the mercy seat of the ark in Exodus chapter twenty-five. God placed cherubim around the tree of life to guard it from Adam and his children, after Adam and Eve sinned, by eating from the tree of knowledge. The description of these living creatures may represent the attributes of Jesus. 1.) The first creature was like a lion. The lion is the most feared creature, and is called the king of all beast. 2.) The second creature was like a calf or an ox. The ox is the strongest of the creatures and the bearer of burdens by man. 3.) The third creature has a face of a man. Man is the most intelligent of all the creatures. 4.) The fourth creature was like a flying eagle. The eagle soars in the air above all creatures.

Vs 8 **"And the four beast had each of them six wings about him; and they were full of eyes within: and they rest not day and night, saying, Holy, Holy, Holy, Lord God Almighty, which was, and is, and is to come."**

The purpose of these living creatures is to continually praise Jesus. Isaiah 6:1-3 **"In the year that king Uzziah died I saw also the Lord sitting upon a throne, high and lifted up, and his train filled the temple. Above it stood the seraphim: each one had six wings; with two he covered his face, and with two he covered his feet, and with two he did fly. And one cried unto another, and said, Holy, Holy, Holy, is the Lord of host: the whole earth is full of his glory."**

Vs 9-11 **"And when those beast give glory and honor and thanks to him that sat on the throne, who liveth for ever and ever, the four and twenty elders fall down before him that sat on the throne, and worship him that liveth for ever and ever, and cast their crowns before the throne, saying, thou art worthy, O Lord, to receive glory and honor and power: for thou hast created all things, and for thy pleasure they are and were created."**

The crowns are the rewards for how we have served Jesus, but this picture is that we are not worthy to be honored, because Jesus alone is worthy and the saved in heaven cast their crowns at the feet of Jesus and give him all the praise and honor and glory for what he has done for us on the cross of Calvary.

REVELATION CHAPTER 5

John sees the sealed book with the judgment of God on those left on the earth who have rejected Jesus as their Lord and Savior. This book is a scroll written on a long piece of paper with each section sealed as it was unrolled. As a seal is broken, it could only be read down to the next seal., and there were seven seals.

Vs 1 **"And I saw in the right hand of him that sat on the throne a book written within and on the backside, sealed with seven seals."**

The one sitting on the throne is the first and the last, the alpha and the omega, God our Father. We see that he has a book in his right hand, a picture of the power of God, for to take something from his strongest hand would be impossible.

Vs 2 **"And I saw a strong angel proclaiming with a loud voice, who is worthy to open the book, and to loose the seals thereof?"**

This angel was strong, maybe the archangel Michael, who even fought with Satan in the Old Testament accounts. A decree goes out for who is worthy to come to the throne of God to take the seven sealed book.

Vs 3   **"And no man in heaven, nor in earth, neither under the earth, was able to open the book, neither to look thereon."**

No one could be found worthy in all of heaven, and earth.

Vs 4   **"And I wept much, because no man was found worthy to open and read the book, neither to look thereon."**

John is still in the flesh as he is privileged to stand there to witness the events that are taking place in the future. John says that he wept much, his emotions overcame him because there was not anyone who is worthy. John knew he was not worthy.

Vs 5   **"And one of the elders saith unto me, Weep not: behold, the Lion of the tribe of Judah, the Root of David, hath prevailed to open the book, and to loose the seven seals thereof."**

There is only one that is worthy that can take the book out of the hand from the one that sits on the throne. This elder, one of the twenty-four, that sits around the throne of God, speaks to John to point out the one who is worthy. Note that a man is sought that is worthy. No angel can come and take the book.

Vs 6 **"And I beheld, and lo, in the midst of the throne and the four beast, and in the midst of the elders, stood a Lamb as it had been slain, having seven horns and seven eyes, which are the seven Spirits of God sent forth into all the earth."**

Jesus is pictured by John as a lamb that has been slain, standing in the middle of the throne. Before this, John saw Jesus standing in the middle of the seven golden candlesticks, telling him to write unto the seven churches. John sees Jesus in a different way now in heaven. In Hebrews, Paul gives us the description of Jesus during the church age as our high priest ministering at the throne of God day and night, interceding in behalf of all the true believers. Paul is speaking predominantly to the Jews in Hebrews, showing us that we have a high priest in Jesus Christ that now is superior to the high priest in the temple at Jerusalem, by a superior sacrifice. The priesthood of Jesus is superior in every way. The Jewish priesthood was passed from man to man but now Jesus ministers forever. The Jewish priesthood entered the holy of holies once a year with blood sacrifices offered every year for the people. Jesus has entered the temple in heaven with his own blood as atonement for the sins of the people, once and forever. The Jewish priesthood was limited to one man in one place for access by all the people. Jesus can hear your confession of sins and you prayers at any time or place in the earth. We do not need the priesthood of a man interceding for man when we have a far superior high priest in Jesus Christ. John now sees Jesus as the savior that gave his life for whomever believes in him as their Lord and Savior. John sees seven horns on his head. Horns throughout the Old Testament signified power or kingdoms. The number seven is a complete or perfect number. These horns may symbolize Jesus having all power over all kingdoms. See Daniel 7:7 for example of the horns representing powers. John saw Jesus with seven eyes of the Holy Spirit, that were sent into all the earth. Jesus knows about everything that is going on in the earth. The Holy Spirit is everywhere, and he knows every thought that we think. Nothing can escape the eyes of the Holy Spirit. Matthew 28:18 **"All power is given unto me in heaven and earth."**

Vs 7   **"And he came and took the book out of the right hand of him that sat upon the throne."**

Jesus willingly went to the cross of Calvary to give his life's blood as an atonement for our sins so that He could be counted worthy to take the book from the right hand of God and to make us acceptable to His Father in heaven. John 5:22 **"The Father judgeth no man, but has committed all judgment to the Son."**

Vs 8   **"And when he had taken the book, the four beast and four and twenty elders fell down before the Lamb, having every one of them harps, and golden vials full of odors, which are the prayers of saints."**

Jubilee breaks out in heaven because He is worthy. Each of these have golden vials, or bowls filled with sweet smelling incense which are the prayers of all the saints. Our prayers to Jesus are not forgotten and are like sweet smelling incense to God the Father. Each of these also have harps, ready to sing a song to the Lord.

Vs 9   **"And they sung a new song, saying, Thou art worthy to take the book, and to open the seals thereof: for thou was slain, and hast redeemed us to God by thy blood out of every kindred, and tongue, and people, and nation."**

This is a new song, I believe much like amazing grace, and they play their harps. Those people who do not believe in music in church need to look at this verse. The Christians have been accused of being slaughter house religionist, well maybe they are right, but it is only by the blood of Jesus that a person will get into heaven. Death was the judgment for sin and it was the death of the sinless perfect Jesus Christ that paid the debt for us to be able to enter heaven.

Vs 10 **"And has made us unto our God kings and priest: and we shall reign on the earth."**

At the end of the seven years of tribulation, Jesus is going to carry us back to the earth to rule and reign over this earth for a thousand years. This promise was made to us all through the Bible. We will be kings and priest, ruling over the earth under the theocratic rule of King Jesus. We will see latter that there will be 144,000 Jews left on the earth in the flesh, when we return with Jesus back to this earth. There will be no death, no sickness and perfect peace for one thousand years. These 144,000 Jews will repopulate the earth, and in one thousand years, there will be a great number of people. We will cover this latter.

Vs 11 **"And I beheld, and I heard the voice of many angels round about the throne and the beast and the elders: and the number of them was ten thousand times ten thousand, and thousands of thousands;"**

God promised to faithful Abraham that because of his faith he would have seed as the sand of the sea. Nationally the Jews from Abraham's son Isaac would number like all the sand of the sea. God also promised faithful Abraham that he would have seed as the stars in heaven. Spiritually those that have faith like father Abraham in the promise of God sending his only begotten son to shed his blood for the sins of the world. God requested Abraham to sacrifice his only begotten son on the altar as an example of what God was going to do for all mankind. All mankind is saved the same way, from Adam to the cross, man looked forward to the sacrifice that would come and from the cross to today, we look back to the actual blood of Jesus that was shed for us. This spiritual seed are in this number that John sees around the throne of God. This number is greater than a hundred trillion saved people in heaven.

Vs 12 **"Saying with a loud voice, Worthy is the Lamb that was slain to receive power, and riches, and wisdom, and strength, and honor, and glory, and blessing."**

Note there are seven things Jesus is worthy to receive:

1.) Power

2.) Riches

3.) Wisdom

4.) Strength

5.) Honor

6.) Glory

7.) Blessing

Vs 13 **"And every creature which is in heaven, and on the earth, and under the earth, and such as are in the sea, and all that are in them, heard I saying, blessing, and honor, and glory, and power, be unto him that siteth upon the throne, and unto the Lamb for ever and ever."**

John is speaking here of his own praise unto God and the Lamb. You have to note that there is one group of people not listed. The people on the earth that have been left, do not hear this great praise of all these in heaven. Romans 8:18-23 **"For I reckon that the sufferings of this present time are not worthy to be compared with the glory which shall be revealed in us. For the earnest expectation of the creature waiteth for the manifestation of the sons of God. For the creature was made subject to vanity, not willingly, but by reason of him who hath subjected the same in hope, because the creature itself also shall be delivered from the bondage of corruption into the glorious liberty of the children of God. For we know that the whole creation groaneth and travaileth in pain together until now. And not only they, but ourselves also, which have the first fruits of the Spirit, even we ourselves groan within ourselves, waiting for the adoption, to wit, the redemption of our body."** Sounds like there will be animals in heaven. Maybe that dear pet we had as a child. I know that the Bible says that Jesus will ride on a white horse when he returns to the earth. The whole creation was placed under a curse because of the sin of father Adam, with all creatures , the plant world, and man suffering till the curse is taken away during the thousand year reign of Jesus Christ on this earth.

Vs 14 **"And the four beast said, A-men. And the four and twenty elders fell down and worshipped him that liveth for ever and ever."**

Amen means surely, surely, this praise of Jesus being worthy is true and will come to pass.

REVELATION CHAPTER 6

The Lamb that is worthy to receive the book out of the right hand of Him that sits on the throne opens the book by breaking the first seal.. Six seals are opened in this chapter and chapter seven is an interlude between the sixth and the seventh seal. Breaking each seal in this chapter may seem like the reading of a book, but on the earth these six seals will cover months or even years. I believe the six seals cover the first forty-two months of the tribulation period and opening of the seventh seal begins the last forty-two months of the tribulation.

The four horsemen of the apocalypse:

Vs 1   **"And I saw when the Lamb opened one of the seals, and I heard, as it were the noise of thunder, one of the four beast saying, come and see."**

John is summoned up front to see the judgments on the inhabitants of the earth. One of the beast is speaking to John with a voice like thunder.

FIRST SEAL- THE WHITE HORSE

Vs 2   **"And I saw, and behold a white horse; and he that sat on him had a bow; and a crown was given unto him; and he went forth conquering, and to conquer."**

This rider on a white horse is the anti-Christ coming into power on the earth. He is an imitator or a false Christ as Jesus warns the Israelites in Matthew chapter twenty-four. This Jews are warned by Jesus in Matthew not to believe when the others say that this is the Christ. The nation of Israel will accept this man as the messiah that they are looking to come as a king. He will have all the credentials that the Jews are looking for. I believe he will be a Jew, a descendant of David. This verse also says that a crown is given to him. He rises to the top of the political world. This man does not have any arrows, but he goes forth conquering and planning to conquer. He has the ultimate goal of conquering the whole world. John will cover this latter.

Vs 3   **"And when he had opened the second seal, I heard the second beast say, come and see."**

SECOND SEAL- THE RED HORSE

Vs 4   **"And there went out another horse that was red; and power was given to him that sat thereon to take peace from the earth, and that they should kill one another; and there was given unto him a great sword."**

At some point in the first forty-two months of the tribulation period, the promise of peace by the first rider will develop into a world war. This may be part of the vision in Daniel chapter seven, where the beasts that Daniel saw represented the kingdoms or world powers that would be on the earth till the end of time. Daniel saw the first beast come out of the sea like a great lion and had eagles wings, which represented the first world power of Babylon. The second beast that came out of the sea was like a bear, which represents the next world power of Medi-Persia. The third beast that came out of the sea was like a leopard with four wings, which represented the world power of Greece. The fourth beast that came out of sea was dreadful, terrible, strong and had iron teeth, which represented the Roman empire. This last beast had ten horns which are explained in verse twenty-four. These horns are ten kingdoms and a little horn rises in the middle of the ten, which plucks out three of the ten horns. The last world power will be the same Roman governments under ten kingdoms, where this little horn will rise to power and destroy three of the kingdoms, and the other seven will give all their power to this little horn. This war on the earth may be the anti-Christ taking total control over the earth by destroying three of these kingdoms. This verse says that there was given unto him a great sword. This great sword may destroy three kingdoms, like plucking out a horn from the head of an animal. This war will be very quick, and then the world will fall under the rule of the anti-Christ. John covers this latter.

THIRD SEAL- THE BLACK HORSE

Vs 5   **"And when he had opened the third seal, and I beheld, and lo a black horse; and he that sat on him had a pair of balances in his hand."**

Following this war, there is a famine in the earth. The food supplied to the world will be destroyed in this war. I do not believe the United States will be a world power during this time. If the food production from the United States were totally cut off from the world, then there would be a famine in the world. During a war, the planting and harvesting would stop.

Vs 6   **"And I heard a voice in the midst of the four beast say, A measure of wheat for a penny, and three measures of barley for a penny, and see thou hurt not the oil and the wine."**

A penny or deaneries was a days wage in Johns day. A man will work one day to earn enough to buy just enough wheat to make a small loaf of bread. A measure of wheat was the ration of wheat given to a Roman soldier each day. The poor will have a hard time just living during this time. The wealthy will not suffer, they will still have their wine and oil to live in luxury. The oil is a necessity today for operating the automobiles, airplanes, electrical plants and industries, but the poor cannot eat oil.

Vs 7   **"And when he had opened the fourth seal, I heard the voice of the fourth beast say, come and see."**

FOURTH SEAL- THE PALE HORSE

Vs 8   **"And I looked, and behold a pale horse: and his name that sat on him was Death, and Hell followed with him. And power was given unto them over the fourth part of the earth, to kill with sword, and with hunger, and with death, and with the beast of the earth."**

There will be a war, then there will be famine and then pestilence. A great number of people will die during this time in the tribulation. John sees one fourth of the worlds population is killed under this horseman alone. The hunger is so bad that men kill each other for food and death is so prevalent that decease spreads everywhere. Even the animals are effected by this famine that they even kill men for food.

FIFTH SEAL

Vs 9   **"And when he had opened the fifth seal, I saw under the altar the souls of them that were slain for the word of God, and for the testimony which they held:"**

All through Revelation, we are reminded that in order to be saved during the tribulation period, a person will give his life as a testimony of their faith. During the church age it has been easy for us to have faith in Jesus Christ and not suffer great persecution for our faith. Those who accept Jesus during the tribulation times will be persecuted greater than any time in history. One reason will be that the Holy Spirit will be removed from the earth so that Satan and his anti-Christ and false prophet can do what they will on this earth. The only thing that prevents Satan from gaining control and causing great persecution to the saved today is the Holy Spirit. In order for a person to be saved then will be for him to not deny Jesus as his Lord and Savior and not deny the Bible as being God's Word. In order to receive the mark of the beast and stay alive, all people will have to bow down and worship the anti-Christ as their god and deny Jesus Christ and the Bible. They will give their life for their testimony.

Vs 10 **"And they cried with a loud voice, saying, How long, O Lord, holy and true, dost thou not judge and avenge our blood on them that dwell on the earth."**

Remember the rapture of all the dead and the remaining Christians on the earth has already happened, and these people under the altar in heaven were not in the rapture. They are soul and spirit, without a regenerated body. This is the same state that all the dead are right now in heaven, waiting for the rapture. They are crying out for revenge against those on the earth, that killed them.

Vs 11 **"And white robes were given to every one of them: and it was said unto them, that they should rest yet for a little season, until their fellow servants also and their brethren, that should be killed as they were, should be fulfilled."**

We will see a little farther along in Revelation that there will be two witnesses sent from heaven to preach day and night for forty-two months on the earth and a lot of people will believe the message of Jesus Christ and not believe the lies of the false prophet and the anti-Christ. These folks under the altar are some of the ones saved by the preaching of the two witnesses. At the middle of the tribulation, God will finally allow Satan to kill these two witnesses and this will begin the final forty-two months of the judgment of God on them that dwell on the earth. White robes are given to every one of them under the altar in heaven. They will be soul and spirit in white robes. There will others killed the same way they were killed in the last forty-two months, but they will also have to give their life as a testimony of their faith. I believe the majority of those saved after the middle of the tribulation will be Jews. When the anti-Christ sits in the holy of holies in the temple in Jerusalem, the nation of Israel will know that this is not the Christ they were looking for, and the Bible tells us that the nation of Israel will saved in a day. When the Jews reject Satan's anti-Christ, he will pursue them and will try to kill all the Jews. Matthew chapter twenty-four describes this time of the Jews being pursued and hunted down to be killed by the anti-Christ. All but 144,000 Jews will be killed, and God will seal them with his seal in their forehead and protect them till the end of the tribulation (Revelation chapter seven). The Jews that will be killed during the last forty-two months of the tribulation are these brethren that should be killed like those under the altar.

<u>SIXTH SEAL</u>

Vs 12 **"And I beheld when he had opened the sixth seal, and lo, there was a great earthquake; and the sun became black as sackcloth of hair, and the moon became as blood."**

This earth will be shaken like it has never been shaken before. God will try to get the attention of those on the earth. Remember Saint Helen, that will be a small sample of what will happen at this time. The cloud of dust will blank out the sun on the earth. This is the final warning from God before the seventh seal is broken by Jesus, and the series of seven bowl judgments are poured out on the earth.

Vs 13 **"And the stars of heaven fell unto the earth, even as a fig tree casteth her untimely figs, when she is shaken of a mighty wind."**

I do not believe this is referring to actual stars in heaven falling on the earth. What I believe the stars represent are the fallen stars are cast onto the earth. The fallen stars that followed Satan in his rebellion against God in heaven are the fallen angels. Revelation 12:3-9 may be the explanation of this verse.

Jesus is going to pull Satan's wings and cast him onto the earth to walk like other men. Satan is called the prince of the power of the air in Ephesians 2:2. Satan has access to heaven right now, accusing us day and night before God in heaven Revelation 12:10. At the middle of the tribulation, Jesus will cast Satan and his angels down to the earth.

Vs 14 **"And the heaven departed as a scroll when it is rolled together; and every mountain and island were moved out of their places."**

This scroll that is rolled up is like shutting the book. The Book that is shut up is the lambs book of life that has the names of every person written in it. If a persons name has been blotted out, then the only way to have it written back in is through believing in Jesus as their Lord and Savior. At the middle of the tribulation all the people on the earth will have been forced to receive the mark of the beast in order to live or reject the mark and refuse to deny Jesus Christ and the Word of God and give their life as their testimony of their faith. This scroll for access to heaven is closed. Under the sixth seal when the earth is shaken by this mighty earthquake, every mountain and island is moved out of their place. Some of these mountains will fall down and some of the islands will just sink into the ocean.

Vs 15 **"And the kings of the earth, and great men, and the rich men, and the chief captains, and every free man, hid themselves in dens and in the rocks of the mountains;"**

The men on this earth at this time of the tribulation will fall down in fear and trembling at the power of God's judgment, but the book of life has been shut, it is to late to accept Jesus, but all them that have the mark of the beast are already doomed to hell Revelation 14:9.

Vs 16 **"And said to the mountains and rocks, fall on us, and hide us from the face of him that siteth on the throne, and from the wrath of the Lamb."**

Those men listed in verse fifteen know God's judgment is coming on them. A great number of people have already been killed by the first six seals, but when the seventh seal is opened, God will pour out his judgment in rapid succession upon the inhabitant on the earth all the way to the end of the last forty-two months.

Vs 17 **"For the great day of his wrath is come; and who shall be able to stand?"**

These same men have heard the two witnesses preach for forty-two months and have heard the gospel message, but have rejected Jesus Christ. They know what is going to happen now, because they have been warned and they refused to listen. Many have sat in churches during the church age and heard preachers tell them about Jesus and they refused to listen. Many will come from the apostate church during the first part of the tribulation and believe they are saved by their being baptized as a baby in the church or their good works they have done or their membership in the church. All these things are what Paul referred to as the religious sinner in Romans 2:17-29.

REVELATION CHAPTER 7

Six seals have been broken by Jesus Christ, the Lamb that is worthy, and in chapter seven John inserts a break between the sixth and seventh seals. John sees the remnant of 144,000 Jews sealed with the seal of God. There are several interpretations as to who the 144,000 will be, but in this chapter John reveals plainly that the remnant will be 12,000 from the twelve tribes of Israel. Paul explains the mystery of iniquity in II Thessalonians 2:1-12. The Holy Spirit will be taken out of this world and then the son of perdition, the anti-Christ will be free to exalt himself as God and sit in the holy of holies in the temple in Jerusalem. This will reveal to the Jews that he is not God and will turn to Jesus Christ as the messiah that they had rejected almost two thousand years earlier. The Jews will believe the anti-Christ is the messiah they are looking for, until he desecrates the holy of holies and proclaims himself as God. This mystery of iniquity will cause the whole nation of Israel to become God's righteous remnant left on the earth during the tribulation period. Romans 11:25-27 tells us of this day when the nation of Israel shall be saved. In Matthew 24:3-31 Jesus himself tells us the events that John is seeing here in Revelation. Vs 31 **"And he shall send his angels with a great sound of a trumpet, and they shall gather together his elect from the four winds, from one end of heaven to the other."** God will not let his judgment on the unrighteous fall upon his elect 144,000 Jews. All the judgments that are about to fall upon the inhabitants on the earth will not harm those who wear the seal of God. Much like the Passover blood of the lamb that was placed above the doors of the houses of the children of Israel in Egypt. The seal of God will protect those who wear it. God's judgment against Egypt in killing the first born of all of Egypt by his death angel, did not have any effect on those who had the lambs blood over their doors. After the sealing of the 144,000 Jews, all the people on the earth will wear either the mark of the beast or the mark of God.

Vs 1   **"And after these things I saw four angels standing on the four corners of the earth, holding the four winds of the earth, that the wind should not blow on the earth, nor on the sea, nor on any tree."**

This event may occur in the middle of the tribulation period, between the opening of the seventh seal and the sixth seal. The picture John sees is as if the angels have stopped the world from turning and time stands still, while the 144,000 Jews are sealed with the seal of God. Revelation 12:13-17 explains the time frame and nation of Israel being saved, having the testimony of Jesus Christ. This will be explained latter on in this book.

Vs 2   **"And I saw another angel ascending from the east, having the seal of the living God; and he cried with a loud voice to the four angels, to whom it was given to hurt the earth and the sea,"**

This seal of God will be placed in the foreheads of the remnant. This angel is sent down to the earth while John sees the winds standing still.

Vs 3   "Saying, Hurt not the earth, neither the sea, nor the trees, till we have sealed

the servants of our God in their foreheads."

After these 144,000 Jews are sealed, the judgments of God on this earth

will fall in rapid succession. God's elect will not suffer from what is about to

happen to those who wear the mark of the beast.

Vs 4   "And I heard the number of them which were sealed: and there were sealed

a hundred forty and four thousand of the tribes of the children of Israel."

There are exactly 144,000 sealed. Not one more or one less, and all were

of the tribes of the children of Israel.

Vs 5-8   "Of the tribe of Judah were sealed twelve thousand, and of the tribe of

Reuben were sealed twelve thousand, of the tribe of Gad were sealed twelve

thousand, of the tribe of Asher were sealed twelve thousand, of the tribe of

Naphtali were sealed twelve thousand, of the tribe of Manasseh were sealed

twelve thousand, of the tribe of Simeon were sealed twelve thousand, of the

tribe of Levi were sealed twelve thousand, of the tribe of Isschar were sealed

twelve thousand, of the tribe of Zebulum were sealed twelve thousand, of the

tribe of Joseph were sealed twelve thousand, of the tribe of Benjamin were

sealed twelve thousand."

You will note that the tribe of Dan has been substituted with the tribe of Menasseh. Genesis 48:8-22 may explain the reason for both the younger and the elder sons of Joseph being blessed by father Israel with a double portion over the other eleven sons. Also you may notice that the tribe of Levi is included, due to the end of the priesthood, when Jesus Christ died on the cross of Calvary. There are some of the tribes of Israel that have been lost since the rebirth of the nation of Israel in 1948. There is a world wide search today by the Jews, trying to find the descendants of all the tribes. Notice also that these tribes are referred to as children of Israel. In Revelation 14:1-5 we will see that these 144,000 Jews were virgins, and they worshipped Jesus as their Lord. They very well may be children when God seals them in their foreheads.

Vs 9 **"After this I beheld, and lo, a great multitude, which no man could number, of all nations, and kindreds, and people, and tongues, stood before the throne, and before the Lamb, clothed with white robes, and palms on their hands;"**

Remember in chapter six and verse eleven, those under the altar that cried out for justice on them on the earth for killing them for their testimony? Now there are some more with them that have come out of the tribulation and have been given white robes.

Vs 10-12 **"And cried with a loud voice, saying, Salvation to our God which siteth upon the throne, and unto the Lamb. And all the angels stood round about the throne, and about the elders and the four beast, and fell before the throne on their faces, and worshipped God. Saying, Amen: Blessing, and glory, and wisdom, and thanksgiving, and honor, and power, and might, be unto our God for ever and ever, Amen."**

The scene was on the earth where the 144,000 Jews were sealed, and now the scene changes back to heaven. The picture is around the throne, where these who have come out of the tribulation period are clothed in white robes, and they are a multitude of people from every nation and race. These people are spirit and soul without a resurrected body. They will receive their resurrected body at the end of the tribulation period and rule and reign on the earth with Christ for a thousand years. Revelation 20:4-6 explains that they will be part of the first resurrection and will be given a resurrected body when Jesus returns to the earth for the thousand year reign on the earth. The rest of the dead or those who have rejected Jesus Christ as their Lord and Savior will be in the second resurrection of the dead at the end of the thousand year reign who will stand at the great white throne judgment and be cast into hell for eternity. There is a great multitude of people who fall on their faces and worship God who sits on the throne.

Vs 13 **"And one of the elders answered, saying unto me, what are these which are arrayed in white robes? And whence came they?"**

Remember John has been carried from the first century into the future to witness the end of time. Maybe this elder is John in the future, asking himself questions, in order to explain what he is seeing. John does not understand everything he is seeing and is describing things in comparison to what he knows. He has never seen an airplane, or electricity and many twentieth century things we accept as common knowledge.

Vs 14 **"And I said unto him, Sir, thou knowest, And he said unto me, These are they which came out of great tribulation, and have washed their robes, and made them white in the blood of the Lamb."**

All people are saved by the blood of the Lamb, from Adam to the very last person saved during the tribulation period. Adam and Eve were shown by God that a blood sacrifice had to be made for atonement of their sins, and they were looking to the future by faith in God's promise of a messiah or the Lamb of God. We today are saved by the very same faith in the blood of the Lamb of God, Jesus Christ. Hebrews chapter nine explains that without the shedding of blood there is no forgiveness of sin. These people have not only given their own life's blood as their testimony by not denying Jesus Christ and his shed blood for them on the

cross of Calvary.

Vs 15 **"Therefore are they before the throne of God, and serve him day and night in**

his temple: and he that siteth on the throne shall dwell among them."

They are in the spirit till chapter twenty when they receive their

resurrected body. John explains here what these tribulation saints will receive for

their faith and sacrifice that they made for Jesus during their life on the earth

during the tribulation period. For eternity these tribulation saints will dwell

around the throne of God

Vs 16 **"They shall hunger no more, neither thirst any more; neither shall the sun**

light on them, nor any heat."

During the tribulation and the first six seals are broken and the four

horses ride out in judgment on the earth. There will be war on the earth with the

red horse, then there will be famine on the earth with the black horse, and then

there will be pestilence on the earth with the pale horse. These people that are

saved during the first half of the tribulation will suffer great hunger and thirst and

heat from the sun by the judgments that fall on the earth. There is a promise

made unto them that they will never have to suffer these things again.

Vs 17 **"For the Lamb which is in the midst of the throne shall feed them, and shall lead them unto living fountains of waters: and God shall wipe away all tears from their eyes."**

When we suffer for the cause of Christ on this earth, we will be rewarded in heaven for enduring what we have on the earth. Romans 5:3-5 **"And not only so, but we glory in tribulation also: knowing that tribulation worketh patience; and patience, experience; and experience, hope; and hope maketh not ashamed; because the love of God is shed abroad in our hearts by the Holy Ghost which is given unto us."** Paul reminds us that we should glory in tribulation because the more tribulation we suffer for the cause of Jesus Christ, the more experience we have seeing God deliver us and bear us through those tribulations. The more experience that we have suffering tribulation builds our faith and hope stronger and stronger till we are able to endure all of life's obstacles that comes our way. We know whatever befalls us in life God will deliver us and reward us in heaven far greater than we ever suffer for Christ sake on this earth.

REVELATION CHAPTER 8

John has revealed the opening of the first six seals of the scroll by Jesus as the Lamb that was slain and who is worthy to take the scroll out of the right hand of him that sits on the throne in heaven. John has revealed to us that there is a great number of people who have been killed for their testimony of Jesus Christ during the tribulation who have been given white robes and are around the throne of God and the Lamb and the four beast and the twenty-four elders. John has revealed that the remnant of 144,000 Jews on the earth have been sealed with the seal of God. Now those who remain on the earth are those people who wear the mark of the beast and those who wear the seal of God. The destiny of all who remain on the earth at this point in time is determined by which seal they wear. Those with the mark of the beast are destined to be judged because they have followed the anti-Christ and rejected Jesus Christ as their Lord and Savior and those with the seal of God are destined to be preserved to the end of the tribulation and protected by God from the persecution of the anti-Christ on the earth. The events from this point on till the end of the last forty-two months of the tribulation period are a series of seven judgments in rapid succession on those that wear the mark of the beast. When the seventh seal is broken and the judgments are proclaimed by Jesus, there is a silence in heaven for thirty minutes. What is going to happen to those who wear the mark of the beast is so terrible that no one in heaven even speaks a word. I imagine that they stand there with their mouths open in horror for those who have rejected Jesus Christ and are ultimately destined for eternal judgment in hell. This time of judgment will be only a taste of what is in store for them in eternity to come.

MOORE ABOUT REVELATION

Romans 1:18 to 2:9 reveals to man that God is a just God and has placed a light in every man to show him there is a God. Man has suppressed that light and explained away the creation that reveals God mighty hand in his creation. Man has rejected the message of his Son Jesus Christ and rather seeking righteousness, has sought unrighteousness. For God will render unto every man according to his deeds. Man will claim that God has shown partiality to the Jew and has called men all through time to be his servants. Like the calling of the twelve apostles, Jesus chose them to follow him and take his message of salvation to the world, but not all accepted the calling. Judas rejected Jesus as God's Son and the Bible tells us that he was not one of Jesus disciples. Romans 9:4 through 10:13 reveals to man that God chose a people to carry his message to the world and he chose a people to bring his Son into the world. Is God unrighteous to allow man to do as he wishes and to be judged for his decision to follow after unrighteousness and to some men God called for a special purpose. Romans 9:20-21 **"Nay but. O man, who art thou that repliest against God? Shall the thing formed say to him that formed it, Why hast thou made me thus? Hath not the potter power over the clay, of the same lump to make one vessel unto honor, and another unto dishonor?"** The potter takes the same lump of clay and divides it into two pieces. One he makes into a beautiful vase to put flowers into it and places it into the church sanctuary to bring honor unto God. The other piece of the same clay, he makes into a spittoon, rough and unfinished, and places it in a bar for men to spit into. It is the same piece of clay and the potter chooses to make one to bring honor and the other to be used as whatever it happens to become. God takes the same flesh and one he uses to bring

honor unto his name and the other he allows to do just as he wishes to bring dishonor and

to even blaspheme his name. God revealed himself to Pharaoh in the miracles and

message by Moses in order to free his people in Egypt. Pharaoh hardened his heart and

refused to accept the message of Moses and free the Israelites. Not all who are called by

God accept his calling. God choose Pharaoh to bring honor and glory to God, but

Pharaoh rejected the calling of God. God has a law that unrighteousness must be judged

and all who have rejected him and the message of the Lamb of God that takes away the

sin of the world will give an account for their unrighteousness. All the people on the

earth at the opening of the seventh seal will have had their opportunity to accept Jesus

Christ or accept the mark of the beast, therefore sealing their destination for eternity.

SEVENTH SEAL-THE JUDGMENT OF GOD

Vs 1   **"And when he had opened the seventh seal, there was silence in heaven about**

      the space of half an hour."

The first half of the tribulation is referred to by Jesus as the "time of

sorrows" in Matthew 24:3-14 and the last half of the tribulation is referred to as

the "great tribulation" by Jesus in Matthew 24:15-29. This great tribulation is

revealed in the opening of the seventh seal.

Vs 2   **"And I saw the seven angels which stood before God; and to them were given seven trumpets."**

In the old testament days the trumpet was used to call the people together for an announcement by the king and to send messages to the armies for the attack. These trumpets announce the judgments on the inhabitants on the earth.

Vs 3   **"And another angel came and stood at the altar, having a golden censer; and there was given unto him much incense, that he should offer it with the prayers of all saints upon the golden altar which was before the throne."**

This angel performs the position of high priest ministering at the altar before the throne of God. Hebrews teaches that Jesus is our high priest ministering in our behalf at the altar in heaven day and night. This angel may be Jesus himself taking the prayers of all the saints in time and offering them upon the altar in heaven and these prayers are like a sweet smelling incense to him that sits on the throne. Notice that the censer is gold in heaven and the censer in the temple on earth was brass.

Vs 4   **"And the smoke of the incense, which came with the prayers of the saints, ascended up before God out of the angel's hand."**

These prayers may be the prayers of those that are killed for their testimony during the tribulation period. Under the sixth seal there is a cry of judgment upon those on the earth that have been killed for their testimony for Jesus Christ during the tribulation. These prayers are now being answered with the Judgment of God upon those who wear the mark of the beast on the earth.

Vs 5 **"And the angel took the censer, and filled it with fire of the altar, and cast it into the earth: and there were voices, and thunderings, and lightnings, and an earthquake."**

Jesus must be this angel to carry out judgment upon the earth. Jesus was offered as a sacrifice on the cross of Calvary and now the sacrifice is falling as judgment upon those who have rejected the sacrifice. This is the beginning of the seven trumpet judgments on the earth.

Vs 6 **"And the seven angels which had the seven trumpets prepared themselves to sound."**

THE FIRST TRUMPET

Vs 7 **"The first angel sounded, and there followed hail and fire mingled with blood, and they were cast upon the earth: and the third part of trees was burnt up, and all green grass was burnt up."**

The angel, Jesus, takes the censer of fire from the altar where the blood of Jesus was offered for the atonement of sin and cast it upon the earth. After Jesus was crucified on the cross and rose from the dead on the third day, he was seen by Mary Magdalene. John 20:17 **"Jesus saith unto her, touch me not; for I am not yet ascended to my Father; but go to my brethren, and say unto them, I ascend unto my Father, and your Father; and to my God, and your God."** Jesus is now our high priest and in tradition of the high priest had to be cleansed before entering the holy of holies to offer up the blood sacrifice on the altar in the temple. Jesus gathered the blood he shed on the cross and delivered it to the altar in heaven to be offered for the sins of the entire world. He could not be defiled before he ascended to his Father to offer up his blood as our high priest in the temple in heaven. Now this blood on the altar in heaven is being cast onto the earth in judgment on those who have rejected the very same blood.

THE SECOND TRUMPET

Vs 8 **"And the second angel sounded, and as it were a great mountain burning with fire was cast into the sea: and the third part of the sea became blood;"**

Another censer of fire from the altar was cast into the sea, and a third of all the seas became blood. If the Bible says that it was blood, then it was blood. I heard a man say one time if the Bible says it, I believe it, and that settles it. You can leave out the middle part and say if the Bible says it, that settles it.

Vs 9 **"And the third part of the creatures which were in the sea. and had life, died; and the third part of the ships were destroyed."**

This judgment is similar to the second bowl judgment in Revelation 16:3. It is going to get hot on this earth. Death is coming to many of the inhabitants on the earth and the smell of death will be everywhere. Commerce on the sea is going to almost stop. It will be hard for the oil cargo ships to deliver their products to the countries. The pleasure ships will be out of business. There will be no pleasure for the inhabitants on the earth after this.

THE THIRD TRUMPET

Vs 10 **"And the third angel sounded, and there fell a great star from heaven, burning as it were a lamp, and it fell upon the third part of the rivers, and upon the fountains of waters;"**

This star falls from heaven and is on fire. We have seen what happens to a meteorite or a satellite when it falls into the atmosphere of the earth. It burns in the oxygen atmosphere as it falls and pieces of this star will fall on a third part of all the drinking water of the earth. Man will already be scorched by the first two trumpet judgments and now they will not have any water to drink.

Vs 11 **"And the name of the star is called Wormwood: and the third part of the waters become wormwood; and many men died of the waters, because they were made bitter."**

This star's name is called Wormwood, because it turned the water bitter. This may be a literal star or meteorite, but it may also be a censer filled with the incense from the altar in heaven that is cast onto the earth's fresh waters. Either way, the fresh water is made bitter and many died from drinking it. They are so thirsty that they drink it any way.

THE FOURTH TRUMPET

Vs 12 **"And the fourth angel sounded, and the third part of the sun was smitten, and the third part of the moon, and the third part of the stars; so as the third part of them was darkened, and the day shone not for a third part of it, and the night likewise."**

The sun will only shine for a third part of the day and the moon will shine only a third part of the night. This is similar to the fourth bowl judgment in Revelation 16:8 where the sun will be turned up to scorch men with heat. If you can imagine the sun only shinning for a third part of the day, it will be very cold on the earth. One third of the earth has burned up and now the earth turns cold. Latter in chapter sixteen, they will burn up with heat.

Vs 13 **"And I beheld, and heard an angel flying through the midst of heaven, saying with a loud voice, Woe, woe, woe, to the inhabitants of the earth by reason of the other voices of the trumpet of the three angels, which are yet to sound."**

Heaven in this verse may refer to the air of the earth, in which all the inhabitants on the earth hear this angel all over the world. This air is referred to as the heavens in Genesis 1:20, Genesis 7:11, Genesis 8:2, and Genesis 27:28. The angel flies around the earth proclaiming three woe's are left for the inhabitants on the earth. If the inhabitants of the earth think what has happened so far is bad, just wait for the rest of the judgments of God.

REVELATION CHAPTER 9

THE FIFTH TRUMPET

THE FIRST WOE

Vs 1   **"And the fifth angel sounded, and I saw a star fall from heaven unto the earth: and to him was given the key of the bottomless pit."**

Under the sixth seal we saw the stars of heaven fall unto the earth and explained that this may be the fallen angels that followed Satan when he rebelled against God in heaven. Jude 6 **"And the angels which kept not their fist estate, but left their own habitation, he hath reserved in everlasting chains under darkness unto the judgment of the great day."** These angels were the ones that married the daughters of men and giants were born to them on the earth. Because of this and the sins of man became so wicked, God destroyed the earth with the flood. The rest of the angels that rebelled against God and followed Satan were cast unto the earth under the sixth seal and now under this fifth trumpet Satan is cast down to the earth. Isaiah 14:12-15 **"How art thou fallen from heaven, O Lucifer, son of the morning! How art thou cut down to the ground, which didst weaken the nations! For thou hast said in thine heart, I will ascend into heaven, I will exalt my throne above the stars of God: I will sit also upon the mount of the congregation, in the sides of the North: I will ascend above the heights of the clouds; I will be like the most High. Yet thou shalt be brought down to hell, to the sides of the pit."** Notice the number of "I will's" in this passage. Satan's pride became so great that he aspired to become God. The sixth seal and the fifth trumpet may follow very close together. John refers to this star as a him, and the keys to the bottomless pit are given to him. The bottomless pit is where the majority of the fallen angels that followed Satan are chained and bound. II Peter 2:4 **"For if God spared not the angels that sinned, but cast them down to hell, and delivered them into chains of darkness, to be reserved unto judgment."** Satan is cast unto the earth, having no more access to heaven and is given the key to the bottomless pit to loose the fallen angels held there. This event is further explained in Revelation 12:10-13. Satan has access to heaven today where he is accusing the saints day and night before God in heaven.

Vs 2   **"And he opened the bottomless pit; and there arose a smoke out of the pit, as the smoke of a great furnace; and the sun and the air were darkened by reason of the smoke of the pit."**

The bottomless pit is reserved for the fallen angels at this present time. During the thousand year reign the false prophet, the anti-Christ, Satan and his fallen angels will be cast into the bottomless pit. We will cover this in chapter twenty at the beginning of the thousand year reign of Christ on the earth. Satan has no more access to heaven to accuse the saints, partly due to the saints being killed for their testimony and already being in heaven and only those who wear the mark of the beast and those who wear the seal of God are left on the earth.

There is no one to accuse left on the earth. Satan opens the bottomless pit to loose his fallen angels and to reveal just what his ultimate motive for all mankind really is. Satan does not care what happens even to those who worship him on the earth.

Vs 3 **"And there came out of the smoke locust upon the earth: and unto them was given power, as scorpions of the earth have power."**

These locust are described latter. They are given power to inflict great pain upon those who wear the mark of the beast. Satan turns them loose upon the inhabitants on the earth.

Vs 4 **"And it was commanded them that they should not hurt the grass of the earth, neither any green thing, neither any tree; but only those men which have not the seal of God in their foreheads."**

God puts a restriction on these locust, to only torment those who do not wear the seal of God in their foreheads. Locust normally eat everything that is green, but these locust are given power to sting men like a scorpion to inflict great pain.

Vs 5   "And to them it was given that they should not kill them, but that they should

be tormented five months: and their torment was as the torment of a

scorpion, when he striketh a man."

These locust are commanded not to kill men, but torment them for five

months. There must be a great number of them turned loose upon those who

wear the mark of the beast. Their job is to torment men. Satan unleashed them

upon all the inhabitants of the earth, just to cause men to hate God even more.

Satan is called a murderer in John 8:44 **"Ye are of your father the devil, and the**

lust of your father ye will do. He was a murderer from the beginning, and

abode not in the truth, because there is no truth in him. When he speaketh a

lie, he speaketh of his own: for he is a liar, and the father of it." Satan's

ultimate goal is to kill all mankind and to cause them to hate God, and he will try

to get you to believe a lie in order to do this.

Vs 6   "And in those days shall men seek death, and shall not find it; and shall

desire to die, and death shall flee from them."

The torment will be so great that no man will not want to live any longer,

but they cannot die for five months. Men will try to kill themselves, but death

will not come to them.

Vs 7 **"And the shapes of the locust were like unto horses prepared unto battle; and on their heads were as it were crowns like gold, and their faces were as the faces of men."**

John has never seen anything like this, so he describes it in comparison to what he knows. Their shape was like a horse in that day prepared for battle. In that day horses wore armor to protect them from spears and arrows. They also had a golden spikes like a crown on their heads and they had faces like a man. They had something that looked like a nose and a mouth to take air in and two bulges that looked like eyes.

Vs 8 **"And they had hair as the hair of women, and their teeth were as the teeth of lions."**

These locust had long hair that hung down and teeth like unto the teeth of a lion. To say the least, they were a horrible creature to look at. John does not say how big they are.

Vs 9 **"And they had breastplates as it were breastplates of iron; and the sound of their wings was as the sound of chariots of many horses running to battle."**

I have heard locust in large numbers, and they make a lot of noise when they swarm. John also may have seen locust swarm, but this description is of many horses running in a battle. They wore armor breastplates and they had wings which may indicate that they were invincible.

Vs 10 **"And they had tails like unto scorpions, and there were stings in their tails: and their power was to hurt men five months."**

John is describing the locust that has come out of the bottomless pit. The size of these creatures may be the size of locust. They have tails like scorpions that have stings in them like the stings of scorpions. Their shape is like horses and they have armor plates. Their heads had long hair with something like a golden crown. Their faces were like a man, but had teeth like a lion. They have wings that sound like many horses running in a battle. Whatever these creatures are, I do not want to meet one of them. Some believe this to be something like a modern day helicopter war machine, but they come out of the bottomless pit, which does not fit that conclusion. These creatures are alive and have hair and are commanded not to kill men, but to torment them for five months. They are just what John calls them, a swam of locust creatures.

Vs 11 **"And they had a king over them, which is the angel of the bottomless pit, whose name in the Hebrew tongue is Abaddon, but in the Greek tongue hath his name Apollyon."**

This star that is cast onto the earth is called an angel and his name is Abaddon and Apollyon, which is interpreted destroyer. This star can only be Satan himself as we have already covered.

Vs 12 **"One woe is past; and behold, there come two woes more hereafter."**

THE SIXTH TRUMPET

THE SECOND WOE

Vs 13 **"And the sixth angel sounded, and I heard a voice from the four horns of the golden altar which is before God,"**

Horns in the Bible represent great powers or kingdoms. Under the Old Testament worship of God in the temple, the altar had four horns which were smeared with the blood of the sacrifice. The power of God was appeased with the blood sacrifice. These inhabitants on the earth do not have any blood sacrifice atonement to appease the power of God from judging them.

Vs 14 **"Saying to the sixth angel which had the trumpet, loose the four angels which are bound in the great river Euphrates."**

Authority is given by the power of God to loose four angels in this great river. These angels control the water ways on the earth. This is most powerful untamed river in the world and it separates China from the western world.

Vs 15 **"And the four angels were loosed, which were prepared for an hour, and a day, and a month, and a year, for to slay the third part of men."**

God has a timetable and everything operates on his clock. Man may think that he is in control of everything on this earth, but nature continually teaches him that God is still in control. For thirteen months, one day and one hour the water of the river Euphrates is held back by these four angels. This sixth trumpet and the sixth angel that poured out his bowl judgment upon the earth, may coincide. Revelation 16:12 **"And the sixth angel poured out his bowl upon the great river Euphrates; and the water thereof was dried up, that the way of the kings of the east might be prepared."** Under the sixth trumpet one third of all men are killed in this war. Under the sixth bowl judgment the great battle at Armageddon all the remaining men upon the earth that wear the mark of the beast are killed. So the river Euphrates will be dried up again under the sixth bowl judgment to prepare the whole worlds army marching against the remaining 144,000 Jews wearing the seal of God in a place called Armageddon. This war under the sixth trumpet last for thirteen months, one day and one hour.

Vs 16 **"And the number of the army of the horsemen were two hundred thousand thousand: and I heard the number of them."**

We are not told how many soldiers that the anti-Christ has, but the army from the east numbers two million men. China has more than this number of soldiers now and by the previous judgments on the earth will have at least two million left at this battle. John describes them as horsemen.

Vs 17 **"And thus I saw the horses in the vision, and them that sat on them, having breastplates of fire, and of jacinth, and brimstone: and the heads of the horses were as the heads of lions; and out of their mouths issued fire and smoke and brimstone."**

John has never seen modern warfare before and did not know what a jet or a helicopter or a tank was. This could be tanks and helicopters that John sees.

Vs 18 **"By these three, was the third part of men killed, by the fire, and by the smoke, and by the brimstone, which issued out of their mouths."**

John sees one third of the men in this battle killed. The anti-Christ army and the two million man army from the east, could have at least a million men killed. There has been a great portion of the worlds population killed by all the trumpet judgments to this point of the tribulation. Approximately half of the population of the entire world left on the earth after the rapture of the church has died in two and one half years.

Vs 19 **"For their power is in their mouth, and in their tails: for their tails were like unto serpents, and had heads, and with them they do hurt."**

The guns of the tanks may be like serpent tails and the turrets of the tanks may be like the heads of lions. John is obviously looking at modern day warfare.

Vs 20 **"And the rest of the men which were not killed by these plaques yet repented not of the works of their hands, that they should not worship devils, and idols of gold, and silver, and brass, and stone, and of wood: which neither can see, nor hear, nor walk."**

All these plaques on the earth and over half of the population of the earth has been killed, and the men that are left still repented not of worshipping the devil and his idols. We will see later that the two witnesses are preaching in Jerusalem for the first forty-two months of the tribulation period and the inhabitants that are left at this point of time still do not repent and turn to Jesus Christ as their Lord and Savior. They are not even sorry for what they are doing and for following Satan and the anti-Christ.

Vs 21 **"Neither repented they of their murders, nor of their sorceries, nor of their fornication, nor of their thefts."**

The men left on the earth wear the mark of the beast or the seal of God at this point and these men who wear the mark of the beast are not even sorry for what they are doing. They have murdered those who have refused to wear the mark of the beast. They have committed sorceries, communing with spirits of the dead and using drugs. They have committed fornication with each other in sexual acts, not having normal relationships in marriage as God designed us to have. They have committed thefts to gain what they want, no matter who they may hurt in getting what they want. They repented not.

REVELATION CHAPTER 10

There is a break between the sixth and the seventh trumpet, much like the break between the sixth and seventh seal of the book or scroll that Jesus has taken out of the right hand of him that sits on the throne in heaven. This picture John shows us in chapter ten jumps all the way to the end of the tribulation period when Jesus returns to the earth. At the close of chapter nine John has seen the seventh seal broken and seven angels were given seven trumpets. Six of these trumpets have sounded from chapter eight to the end of chapter nine. The first trumpet caused one third of all the trees and grass is burned. The second trumpet caused one third of all the seas to become blood. The third trumpet caused one third of all the fresh water to become bitter. The fourth trumpet caused the sun and the moon not to shine for a third part of the day. The fifth trumpet cast Satan down to the earth and gave him the key to the bottomless pit to loose the hordes of locust upon the men on the earth. The sixth trumpet caused the river Euphrates to dry up and open the way for an army of two million men to war against the anti-Christ and his army. Between the sixth and the seventh seal there was a break where John saw the 144,000 Jews receive the seal of God in their foreheads. That was approximately the midpoint of the seven years of the tribulation period. This break in chapter ten through chapter thirteen is where John goes back to explain many of the things he has seen in more detail. Then in chapter fourteen, John picks back up with Jesus standing on Mount Zion returning to the earth at the end of the seven years of the tribulation period.

Vs 1   **"And I saw another mighty angel come down from heaven, clothed with a**

cloud: and a rainbow was upon his head, and his face was as it were the sun,

and his feet as pillars of fire:"

John describes this mighty angel with the little book:

1.) He is clothed with a cloud. Jesus will return in a cloud. Acts 1:9-11

2.) A rainbow was upon his head. Revelation 4:3

3.) His face was as it were the sun. Revelation 1:16

4.) His feet were as pillars of fire. Revelation 1:15

This mighty angel could be none other than the Lord Jesus Christ. This picture reveals that Jesus is returning in a cloud to the earth in judgment on those who have rejected his shed blood and have received the mark of the beast.

Vs 2   **"And he had in his hand a little book open: and he set his right foot upon the**

sea, and his left foot on the earth,"

The little book is open and also note that all of the seals of the seven sealed scroll have been broken. This may be the same book that he took out of the right hand of him that sits on the throne. Some believe that this is the Bible that is open, representing the word of God. Either way the results are the same. Jesus steps onto the earth and the sea as the King of Kings and Lord of Lords.

Vs 3   **"And cried with a loud voice, as when a lion roareth: and when he had cried, seven thunders uttered their voices."**

Jesus is called the lion of the tribe of Juda all through the Bible. A lion is the mightiest of the beast and when a lion roars, it sends chills down the spine. At the same time seven thunders uttered their voices. Have you ever heard the thunder and seen the lightning at the same time? Well if you have you are lucky to be alive. When this happens, you just do not stand there as if nothing had happened, it will get your attention immediately. These seven thunders get the attention of those who are on the earth.

Vs 4   **"And when the seven thunders had uttered their voices, I was about to write: and I heard a voice from heaven saying unto me, Seal up those things which the seven thunders uttered, and write them not."**

These seven thunders are judgments upon the inhabitants on the earth that John is told not to write about. We do not know what they say or is done to those who wear the mark of the beast on the earth. These judgments are like a roaring lion and must be fierce and vicious like the most feared wild beast on the earth. We would not understand them or they are so fierce that we are not told what they are.

Vs 5-6   **"And the angel which I saw stand upon the sea and upon the earth lifted up**

his hand to heaven, and sware by him that liveth for ever and ever, who

created heaven, and the things that therein are, and the earth, and the things

that therein are, and the sea, and the things which are therein, that there

should be time no longer:"

John has revealed to us that Jesus was in the beginning with God and all

things were created by him. John 1:1-3 **"In the beginning was the Word, and**

the Word was with God, and the Word was God. The same was in the

beginning with God. All things were made by him; and without him was not

any thing made that was made." Jesus lifts up his hand and swears by him that

liveth for ever and ever. Hebrews 6:13 **"For when God made a promise to**

Abraham, because he could swear by no greater, he swear by himself." Here

Jesus swears by him that liveth for ever and ever, or by himself, that there should

be time no longer. This is the end of the time of man on this earth. As pictured in

the introduction of this book, the number of man is six, created on the sixth day of

creation and his time upon this earth is six days or six thousand years. The end of

the six thousand years are fulfilled in this verse and the day of the Lord, or the

thousand year reign is to begin.

Vs 7   "But in the days of the voice of the seventh angel, when he shall begin to

sound, the mystery of God should be finished, as he hath declared to his

servants the prophets."

The apostle Paul explains the mystery of God in Colossians chapter two.

The mystery of how we are saved through the blood of Jesus that was shed on the

cross of Calvary and how we are given an everlasting body just like Jesus Christ,

the firstborn of the dead. Colossians 2:9-15 **"For in him dwelleth all the**

fullness of the Godhead bodily. And ye are complete in him, which is the

head of all principality and power: In whom also ye are circumcised with the

circumcision made without hands, in putting off the body of sins of the flesh

by the circumcision of Christ: Buried with him in baptism, wherein also ye

are risen with him through the faith of the operation of God, who hath raised

him from the dead. And you, being dead in your sins and the uncircumcision

of your flesh, hath he quickened together with him, having forgiven you all

trespasses; Blotting out the handwriting of ordinances that was against us,

which was contrary to us, and took it out of the way, nailing it to his cross;

And having spoiled principalities and powers, he made a show of them

openly, triumphing over them in it." This verse in Revelation is the triumph of

Jesus Christ over all those who have rejected him and followed after sin and

Satan.

Vs 8   "And the voice which I heard from heaven spake unto me again, and said, Go
and take the little book which is open in the hand of the angel which standeth
upon the sea and upon the earth."

This voice that told John not to record the voices of the seven thunders,
now tells John to go and take the little book from the angel, Jesus, that is now
standing on the sea and the earth. This may be God speaking directly to John.

Vs 9-10 "And I went unto the angel, and said unto him, Give me the book. And he
said unto me, Take it, and eat it up; and it shall make thy belly bitter, but it
shall be in thy mouth sweet as honey. And I took the little book out of the
angel's hand, and ate it up; and it was in my mouth sweet as honey: and as
soon as I had eaten it, my belly was bitter."

This little book that is open may represent the actual little book that John
is going to record about the events he has seen and been commanded to write
which will be a little book in the big book the Bible. The book of Revelation is
sweet to the Christian who believes in Jesus Christ as their Lord and Savior, but
when we see the judgment of God on all those who have rejected Jesus, then it
becomes bitter in our belly. All Christians want to see the lost come to Jesus for
salvation, but the awful tragedy is that most of the lost world does not want to be

saved. This causes us to have a bitter feeling in our belly and we sometimes wish there was something more that we could do in leading the lost to Jesus.

Vs 11   **"And he said unto me, thou must prophesy again before many peoples, and nations, and tongues, and kings."**

Jesus tells John that he is not finished with John, even though the Romans have put John on a little island to die, he will live to prophesy a while longer on the earth before Jesus is finished with him. What a privilege John had to see the end of time and then carry this message back to the earth where millions of people will read the accounts of Revelation and trust in Jesus by hearing the inspired Word of God. The little book that was open and John was commanded to eat it up may very well be the fulfillment of this verse of scripture.

REVELATION CHAPTER 11

The break between the sixth and seventh trumpet is like a flashback to things that have already occurred under the seven seals of the scroll. Chapter eleven opens with the temple on the earth and closes with the temple in heaven. From chapter eleven to chapter nineteen John gives us many details and explanations which are the basis for understanding all of the book of Revelation.

THE TEMPLE ON THE EARTH

Vs 1   **"And there was given me a reed like unto a rod: and the angel stood, saying, Rise, and measure the temple of God, and the altar, and them that worship therein."**

This temple is on the earth and will be the fifth temple to be built in Jerusalem. The first temple was built by Solomon and was destroyed by Nebuchadnezzar in 587 BC. The second temple was rebuilt by Zerubbabel and finished in 515 BC. Herod began rebuilding the Zerubbabel temple in 19 BC, which was the third temple and was not completed till around 64 AD. Titus destroyed the third temple in 70 AD Hadrian built a temple to Jupiter Capitolinus in 136 AD on the site of the Herodian temple. The fourth temple was built by Julian around 363 AD but was burned before its completion. Today the Dome of the Rock referred to as the Mosque of Omar is thought to occupy the place where the original temple stood. The Israelites believe the foundations of the original temple lie just outside the Mosque of Omar, and are presently making

plans to rebuild the temple. There may be an earthquake or something to destroy

this Mosque of Omar, which will allow the Israelites to rebuild the temple again.

This final temple on the earth will be rebuilt and is the temple that John is

instructed to measure. The church body, that is every true believer in Jesus Christ

as their Lord and Savior, is the temple today. I Corinthians 3:16 **"Know ye not**

that ye are the temple of God, and that the Spirit of God dwelleth in you."

Vs 2 **"But the court which is without the temple leave out, and measure it not; for**

it is given unto the gentiles: and the holy city shall they tread under foot

forty and two months."

This verse marks the end of times of the gentiles on the earth. The times

of the gentiles is referred to as when the Jews rejected Jesus Christ and his death

on the cross and his shed blood for the remission of their sins and his rising from

the grave victorious over sin, so God turned the gospel message toward the gentile

nations. The Apostle Paul was called to go unto the gentiles to preach the gospel.

For almost two thousand years it has been the times of the gentiles to receive

God's blessings and salvation through their faith in Jesus Christ. This verse gives

us a time table for the end of the times of the gentiles, when God will again turn

his blessings to the Jews and they will accept his Son, Jesus Christ as their

Messiah. For the first forty two months of the tribulation, there will be many gentiles saved and those who wear the mark of the beast will tread the holy city

Jerusalem under their feet up to the end of the forty two months, but not beyond

that point. John is told not to measure the outer court for it is given to the

gentiles. God is beginning to bless the nation of Israel again today, and here

during the tribulation the gentiles are the followers of the anti-Christ. The outer

court is not part of the original plan given to Moses, but was added in the

Herodian temple and will be added to the temple in the tribulation period.

Daniel 7:24-25 **"And the ten horns out of this kingdom are ten kings**

that shall arise: and another shall rise after them; and he shall be diverse

from the first, and shall subdue three kings. And he shall speak great words

against the most High, and shall wear out the saints of the most High, and

think to change times and laws: and they shall be given into his hand until a

time and times and the dividing of time." Daniel prophesied of the anti-Christ

rising to power during a time (a year) and times (two years) and the dividing of

time (a half year). The anti-Christ will rise to great power during the first forty

two months.

THE TWO WITNESSES

Vs 3   **"And I will give power unto my two witnesses, and they shall prophesy a**

thousand two hundred and threescore days, clothed in sackcloth."

Daniel 12:4-7 **"But thou, O Daniel, shut up the words, and seal the book, even to the time of the end: many shall run to and fro, and knowledge shall be increased. Then I Daniel looked, and, behold, there stood other two, the one on this side of the bank of the river, and the other on that side of the bank of the river. And one said to the man clothed in linen, which was upon the waters of the river, How long shall it be to the end of these wonders? And I heard the man clothed in linen, which was upon the waters of the river, when he held up his right hand and his left hand unto heaven, and sware by him that liveth for ever that it shall be for a time, times, and a half; and when he shall have accomplished to scatter the power of the holy people, all these things shall be finished."** We see the entire tribulation period with the two witnesses preaching the gospel message for the first forty two months while the anti-Christ gains total power over the earth and then after the anti-Christ sets himself up as god to be worshipped by all the world, there will another forty two months when Jesus scatters the worshipers of Satan's anti-Christ and then he comes back to this earth in total victory over Satan. The true church or bride of Christ will be taken out at the beginning of the tribulation and there will be two witnesses that will stand in the streets of Jerusalem for forty two months preaching the gospel message day and night. They will be the only ones that are able to stand against Satan to preach the true gospel, all others will be killed for their testimony. It will be open season on all those who profess Christ as their Lord and Savior. Power will be given unto them to do many miracles.

Vs 4   **"These are the two olive trees, and the two candle sticks standing before the**

god of the earth."

Olive oil is the anointing oil which may symbolize they are prophets of the

Lord. They are two candle sticks, which in Revelations 1:20 we saw that the

candle sticks represent the church. These two men will be the only church or

light in this world for the lost people left on this earth to hear the gospel message.

The gospel will be preached for only the first forty two months, which supports

the position that by the time of the last forty two months, all the people who are

going to be saved will have given their life for their testimony and all that are left

on the earth for the last forty two months are those who have received the mark of

the beast and those who have received the seal of God in their foreheads. The

two witnesses stand before the god of the earth, which by this time during the

tribulation period will be the anti-Christ who sits on a throne in the holy of holies

to be worshipped by the world as God. All those who do not fall down and

worship him and receive his mark in their right hand or their forehead will be

killed. There has been much speculation as to who the two witnesses will be,

since we are not told by John. Some say they are Elijah and Moses and some say

Elijah and Enoch. The last words of the Old Testament Malachi 4:1-6 **"For,**

behold, the day cometh, that shall burn as an oven; and all the proud, yea,

and all that do wickedly, shall be stubble: And the day that cometh shall

burn them up, saith the Lord of Host, that it shall leave them neither root nor branch. But unto you that fear my name shall the Sun of righteousness arise with healing in his wings; and ye shall go forth, and grow up as calves of the stall. And ye shall tread down the wicked; for they shall be ashes under the soles of your feet in the day that I shall do this, saith the Lord of Host. Remember ye the law of Moses my servant, which I commanded unto him in Horeb for all Israel, with the statutes and judgments. Behold, I will send you Elijah the prophet before the coming of the great and dreadful day of the Lord: And he shall turn the heart of the fathers to the children, and the heart of the children to the fathers, lest I come and smite the earth with a curse." Now if we look at the plagues that they put upon the earth, then we may conclude that they are similar to the plagues that Moses and Elijah both were given during their life on this earth. In Romans 10:14-21, Paul is speaking of this very time in the tribulation: **"But I say, Have they not heard? Yes verily, their sound went into all the earth, and their words unto the ends of the world. But I say, Did not Israel know? First Moses saith, I will provoke you to Jealousy by them that are no people, and by a foolish nation I will anger you."** Mark 9:2-4 **"And after six days Jesus taketh with him Peter, James and John, and leadeth them up into a high mountain apart by themselves: and he was transfigured before them. And his raiment became shining, exceeding white as snow; so as no fuller on earth can white them. And there appeared** unto them Elijah with Moses; and they were talking with Jesus." The two witnesses must be Elijah and Moses.

Vs 5   "And if any man will hurt them, fire proceedeth out of their mouth, and devoureth their enemies: and if any man will hurt them, he must in this manner be killed."

Elijah caused fire to come down from heaven: II Kings 1:10 **"And Elijah answered and said to the captain of fifty, If I be a man of God, then let fire come down from heaven, and consume thee and thy fifty, and there came down fire from heaven, and consumed him and his fifty."** I Kings 18:38 **"Then the fire of the Lord fell, and consumed the burnt sacrifice, and the wood, and the stones, and the dust, and licked up the water that was in the trench."** Elijah challenged four hundred and fifty prophets of Baal and four hundred prophets of the groves to sacrifice two bulls, one for Baal and one for God. The prophets of Baal chanted all day for Baal to consume their sacrifice and cut themselves, but nothing happened. Elijah at evening time took his bull and grain offering and put it on wood, twelve stones and then wet it down with four barrels of water filled three times. Then Elijah prayed to God and everything was consumed with a fire from heaven.

Vs 6   **"These have power to shut heaven, that it rain not in the days of their**

prophesy: and have power over the waters to turn them to blood, and to

smite the earth with all plagues, as often as they will."

Moses caused plagues and turned water to blood in Egypt, in order to get

Pharaoh to let the Israelites go from their slavery. These two witnesses could

only be Elijah and Moses.

Vs 7   **"And when they shall have finished their testimony, the beast that ascendeth**

out of the bottomless pit shall make war against them, and shall overcome

them, and kill them."

The star or Satan fell from heaven and was given the key to the bottomless

pit under the fifth trumpet. This beast is the anti-Christ, which is loosed out of

the bottomless pit. This beast is described in Revelation chapter thirteen, rising

up out of the sea. The identity of this beast will be given in chapter thirteen. He

is referred to as the son of perdition. Satan is an imitator and may have a human

son the same as God has a Son in Jesus Christ. This man will be identified by

scripture latter. All mankind has a purpose to fulfill on this earth. When we have

served God and fulfilled our purpose, then God will take us home to heaven. The

unrighteous are left on the earth as long as possible for them to hear the word of

God and turn from their sins and trust in Jesus, or sometimes they are left to live out their lives by the mercy of God prolonging the inevitable eternal hell that awaits them. The beast or anti-Christ is finally allowed to kill the two witnesses after preaching forty two months. II Thessalonians 2:3-4 **"Let no man deceive you by any means: for that day shall not come, except there come a falling away first, and the man of sin be revealed, the son of perdition; Who opposeth and exhalteth himself above all that is called God, or that is worshipped; so that he as God sitteth in the temple of God, showing himself that he is God."**

Vs 8   **"And their dead bodies shall lie in the street of the great city, which spiritually is called Sodom and Egypt, where also our Lord was crucified."**

The two witnesses are going to be left where they lie in the street. They have preached Jesus and him crucified for the sins of the world and how he was buried and rose the third day. They will be in the streets just outside the temple, where the Jews will be able to see them and hear them day and night preaching the gospel message. The Revelation of John tells us that they will rise from the dead the third day, and they will be left where they lay to see if they will come back to life. This city, referred to as Sodom and Egypt is Jerusalem, where Jesus was crucified. The name Sodom and Egypt refer to the influence of the anti-Christ who has moved his throne to Jerusalem at the middle of the tribulation period.

Vs 9 **"And they of the people and kindreds and tongues and nations shall see their**

dead bodies three days and a half, and shall not suffer their dead bodies to be

put in graves."

It would have been difficult for us to understand this verse just fifty years

ago, but we can picture the world looking at their television and the news every

hour on the hour showing them still lying in the street. The world in that day

may even remember what the book of Revelation says about these two witnesses

rising from the dead and they have the cameras trained on where they lie, waiting

to prove that John was wrong. Many people today do not believe the book of

Revelation and that John was out of his head when he wrote this book. To deny

that the book of Revelation is relevant to the Christian today is to deny part of

God's holy Word and the scripture that tells us all God's Word is inspired by the

Holy Spirit. Revelation 22:19 **"And if any man shall take away from the words**

of the book of this prophesy, God shall take away his part out of the book of

life, and out of the holy city, and from the things which are written in this

book."

Vs 10 **"And they that dwell upon the earth shall rejoice over them, and make**

merry, and shall send gifts, one to another; because these two prophets

tormented them that dwelt on the earth."

The anti-Christ has claimed to have rid the earth of the two witnesses and his power over them is greater than the two witnesses. The earth is rejoicing and worshipping the anti-Christ for killing them. The world gives great power to the anti-Christ because of his killing the two witnesses. The Anti-Christ may move his kingdom to the temple in Jerusalem during these three days that the two witnesses lie in the street and the world worships the beast as God.

THE SECOND WOE

Vs 11 **"And after three days and a half the spirit of life from God entered into them, and they stood upon their feet; and great fear fell upon them which saw them."**

Romans 11:25-27 **"blindness in part is happened to Israel, until the fullness of the gentiles be come in. And so all Israel shall be saved: as it is written, There shall come out of Zion the Deliverer, and shall turn away ungodliness from Jacob: For this is my covenant unto them, when I shall take away their sins."** This may be the very day spoken of when the entire nation of Israel will turn to Jesus Christ as their Lord and Savior, when they see the two witnesses rise from the dead. The anti-Christ will exalt himself as God and move his throne into the holy of holies in the temple and proclaim to be God after killing the two witnesses. The Jews will see this and the next verse and see that what the two witnesses have been preaching for forty-two months was true.

Vs 12 **And they heard a great voice from heaven saying unto them, come up hither, and they ascended up to heaven in a cloud; and their enemies beheld them."**

The two witnesses are Jews and they have been preaching for forty two months in Jerusalem and the nation of Israel has heard the gospel message and now they believe the two witnesses and reject the anti-Christ. Great fear falls on the world when this happens. The anti-Christ is outraged at the Jew rejection and not falling down to worship him as God and the following events are recorded in Matthew chapter twenty four and Luke chapter twenty one.

Vs 13 **"And the same hour was there a great earthquake, and the tenth part of the city fell, and in the earthquake were slain of men seven thousand: and the remnant were afrightened, and gave glory to the God of heaven."**

God shakes the earth and those who worship the anti-Christ. In the same hour that the two witnesses rise from the dead and ascend into heaven in a cloud, the remnant gives glory to the God of heaven. The remnant is speaking of the Jews that have accepted Jesus Christ as their Lord and Savior. In one hour the nation of Israel turns from the anti-Christ to accept Jesus Christ as their Messiah.

In chapter seven the remnant are sealed with the seal of God after the judgment of the sixth seal and before the opening of the seventh seal. This gives a time frame for the opening of the seventh seal after the first forty-two months of the tribulation. The Israelites will turn to Jesus Christ and give glory to the God of Heaven and not to the god of the earth. This is the beginning of the flight of the Jews mentioned in Matthew chapter twenty four, for they were affrighted not of God, but of the anti-Christ.

Vs 14 **"The second woe is past; and, behold the third woe cometh quickly."**

This event happens at the middle of the tribulation after the first forty two months and may coincide-inside with the opening of the sixth seal in chapter seven with a great earthquake and the stars of heaven falling unto the earth.

THE SEVENTH TRUMPET

Vs 15 **"And the seventh angel sounded; and there were great voices in heaven, saying, The kingdoms of this world are become the kingdom of our Lord, and of the Christ; and he shall reign for ever and ever."**

Satan has the power to give wealth and kingdoms to men on this earth for falling down and worshipping him. Matthew 4:8-9 **"Again, the devil taketh him up into an exceeding high mountain, and showeth him all the kingdoms of the** world, and the glory of them; and saith unto him, All these things will I give thee, if thou wilt fall down and worship me." Satan, even to the very last of the tribulation, desires to be worshipped as God and offered Jesus the entire world if he would just fall down and worship him. At the end of the tribulation period, God declares that this world and all its kingdoms are become the kingdom of our Lord Jesus Christ. The seventh trumpet signals the end of the tribulation and the eminent return of Jesus Christ to the earth as the King of Kings and Lord of Lords. Between the sixth trumpet and the seventh trumpet there will be seven vials or bowls of the wrath of God. Revelation chapter fifteen and sixteen tells us what these seven last plagues are.

Vs 16 **"And the four and twenty elders, which sat before God on their seats, fell upon their faces, and worshipped God."**

John has jumped from the middle of the tribulation period to the end with the preparation of the return of Jesus Christ. A jubilee breaks out in heaven. The scene has switched from the temple on the earth to the temple in heaven.

Vs 17 **"Saying, we give thee thanks, O Lord God Almighty, which art, and wast, and art to come; because thou hast taken to thee thy great power, and hast reigned."**

This verse shows to man that God has a permissive will and allows man to make a choice to whom he will serve. Joshua 24:15 **"And if it seem evil unto you to serve the Lord, choose you this day whom ye will serve; whether the gods which your fathers served that were on the other side of the flood, or the gods of the Amorites, in whose land ye dwell: but as for me and my house, we will serve the Lord."** Man has to choose one way or the other if he will serve God or Satan. When the final day of man's free will ends is when Jesus Christ comes back to this earth to judge man for the decision he has made.

Vs 18 **"And the nations were angry, and thy wrath is come, and the time of the dead, that they should be judged, and that thou shouldest give reward unto thy servants the prophets, and to the saints, and them that fear thy name, small and great: and shouldest destroy them which destroy the earth."**

The anti-Christ and all those who worship him as their god are angry because God's wrath is falling on them and they are being judged for their unrighteousness. Romans 1:18-32 **"For the wrath of God is revealed from heaven against all ungodliness and unrighteousness of men, who hold the truth in unrighteousness; Because that which may be known of God is manifest in them; for God hath showed it unto them. For the invisible things of him from the creation of the world are clearly seen, being understood by the things that are made, even his eternal power and Godhead; so that they** are without excuse: Because that, when they knew God, they glorified him not as God, neither were thankful; but became vain in their imaginations, and their foolish heart was darkened. Professing themselves to be wise, they became fools, And changed the glory of the incorruptible God into an image made like to corruptible man, and to birds, and fourfooted beast, and creeping things. Wherefore God also gave them up to uncleanness through the lust of their own hearts, to dishonor their own bodies between themselves; Who changed the truth of God into a lie, and worshipped and served the creature more than the Creator, who is blessed for ever. Amen. For this cause God gave them up unto vile affections: for even their women did change the natural use into that which is against nature: And likewise also the men, leaving the natural use of the woman, burned in their lust one toward another; men with men working that which is unseemly, and receiving in themselves that recompense of their error which was meet. And even as they did not like to retain God in their knowledge, God gave them over to a reprobate mind, to do those things which are not convenient; Being filled with all unrighteousness, fornication, wickedness, covetousness, maliciousness; full of envy, murder, debates, deceit, malignity; whispers, backbiters, haters of God, despiteful, proud, boasters, inventors of evil things, disobedient to parents, without understanding, covenantbreakers, without natural affection, implacable, unmerciful: Who knowing the judgment of

God, that they which commit such things are worthy of death, not only do the same, but have pleasure in them that do them."

God will judge this world for their decision of serving God or serving Satan and the world is angry because of his judgment. To many times we hear the message of God's love and not the judgment of God. The world needs to know that God hates those things recorded in Romans chapter one, and will judge man for willfully committing those things. The worlds view on many of these things is evidently according to Satan's desire to undermine God's Word and is supported by the world. Homosexuality is something that God hates and is a direct result of rejecting God's Son, Jesus Christ. When man turns his back on the creation and the Bible account of God creating everything, and worships the creation over the creator, then their foolish heart is darkened and they are turned over to a reprobate mind. This is why the world sees nothing wrong with homosexuality and living with each other outside of marriage and even have pleasure in those that support their way of thinking. All those who reject God's way of righteous living will stand in the great white throne judgment in Revelation chapter twenty and be rewarded eternal damnation in hell for their decisions made in this lifetime.

Vs 19 "And the temple of God was opened in heaven, and there was seen in his temple the ark of his testament: and there were lightning's, and voices, and thundering's, and an earthquake, and great hail."

The temple is opened in heaven for access to and from the earth for the righteous and is the preparation for the Lord coming back to this earth with his saints to rule and reign over this earth for a thousand years.

REVELATION CHAPTER 12

Chapter twelve and chapter thirteen records seven explanations of what John has already described and is like a flashback in a movie where John reveals the seventh trumpet and the preparation of Jesus coming back to this earth and then goes back to explain events that have already taken place under the seven seals that have been opened. John explains seven characters that are the basis for understanding most of the symbolism through the entire book of Revelation. The seventh trumpet was blown at the end of chapter eleven which signals the end of the seven years of tribulation, and the explanations and flashback of what John has seen continues to chapter nineteen. Revelation chapter eleven closes with the temple in heaven being opened and continues again in Revelation chapter nineteen and verse eleven, where heaven is opened to let Jesus Christ ride out on a white horse to return to the earth to make war with Satan, the anti-Christ, the false prophet and all those who wear the mark of the beast.

THE FIRST CHARACTER-THE WOMAN

Vs 1   **"And there appeared a great wonder in heaven; a woman clothed with the sun, and the moon under her feet, and upon her head a crown of twelve stars."**

This is not a literal woman, but represents the nation of Israel from Jacob, who was latter renamed by God as Israel, who fathered twelve sons to the end of time. The youngest son of Israel was Joseph and was loved more than the other eleven sons. Joseph had a dream in which he was the chosen seed through which the messiah would come into this world. Genesis 37:3-11 **"Now Israel loved Joseph more than all his children, because he was the son of his old age: and he made him a coat of many colors. And when his brethren saw that their father loved him more than all his brethren, they hated him, and could not speak peaceably unto him. And Joseph dreamed a dream, and he told it his brethren: and they hated him yet the more. And he said unto them, Hear, I pray you, this dream which I have dreamed: For, behold, we were binding sheaves in the field, and, lo, my sheaf arose, and also stood upright; and, behold, your sheaves stood around about, and made obeisance to my sheaf. And his brethren said unto him, Shalt thou indeed reign over us? And they hated him yet the more for his dreams, and for his words. And he dreamed yet another dream, and told it his brethren, and said, Behold, the sun and the moon and the eleven stars made obeisance to me. And he told it to his father, and to his brethren: and his father rebuked him, and said unto him, what is this dream that thou hast dreamed? Shall I and thy mother and thy brethren indeed come to bow down ourselves to thee to the earth? And his brethren envied him; but his father observed the saying."** The sun represented Israel, the moon represented his mother and the eleven stars represented his brothers. This woman in Revelation represents the nation of Israel. Through the lineage of Joseph the Messiah was born through the seed of the woman. Notice also that the promise of the Messiah was promised to come through Eve's seed. Genesis 3:15-

16 **"And I will put emmity between thee and the woman, and between thy seed and her seed; it shall bruise thy head, and thou shalt bruise his heel. Unto the woman he said, I will greatly multiply thy sorrow and thy conception; in sorrow thou shalt bring forth children; and thy desire shall be to thy husband, and he shall rule over thee."** The promised Messiah was through the seed of woman and not of man which speaks of the virgin birth of Jesus Christ. Notice that the promise of God was between the seed of Satan and the seed of the woman and that the head of the seed of Satan will be bruised by the heal of the seed of the woman. This will be covered in more detail in chapter thirteen.

Vs 2 **"And she being with child cried, travailing in birth, and pained to be delivered."**

The woman, Israel, travailed in birth and the pains continued after the birth of her child. This verse is direct result of the promise God made to Eve in childbearing but the continuation of the pains from the birth is the effort of Satan to persecute the woman. Because the woman brought forth the man child that God promised to Eve, all the Israelites are hated by Satan and has been the object of his persecution all through history. Hitler, for example, was an instrument of Satan in persecuting the woman during World War II. The hatred of Israel by the Arab countries today is a direct result of Satan's persecution of the woman.

THE SECOND CHARACTER- THE GREAT RED DRAGON

Vs 3   **"And there appeared another wonder in heaven; and behold a great red dragon, having seven heads and ten horns, and seven crowns upon his heads."**

This beast with the seven heads and ten horns and seven crowns will be described in detail in chapter seventeen. This also is the beast that rises out of the sea in chapter thirteen. The characteristics of this great red dragon are the same characteristics of the beast that rises out of the sea. The explanation of the similarity may be that the trinity of Satan exhibit the same characteristics. Satan is a trinity, Satan, the anti-Christ and the false prophet or Satan the father, Satan the son and Satan the spirit. They are all the same. The beast that rises out of the sea is the anti-christ and may be the same man Jesus refered to as the son of perdition that rises up out of the bottomless pit. Revelation 17:8 **"The beast that thou sawest was, and is not; and shall asend out of the bottomless pit, and go into perdition: and they that dwell on the earth shall wonder, whose names were not written in the book of life from the foundation of the world, when they behold the beast that was, and is not, and yet is."**

Characteristics of Satan:

1.) <u>This beast is great</u>. Great power is given unto the beast that rises out of the sea by Satan to do great wonders before the world. The world will give him great power as a dictator ruling over them with absolute control.

2.) <u>This beast is red</u>. Satan was a murderer from the beginning and the color of the beast reflects his father. He is just like his father.

3.) <u>This beast is called a dragon</u>. He is vicious in nature. Satan used Herod to try to kill the baby Jesus by killing all the male children two years old and younger for a hundred mile radius from Jerusalem. Satan also used Pilate and Herod's son to crucify the innocent Jesus Christ, thinking that he had finally killed the very Son of God. Three days latter, the victory was all God's, when Jesus Christ rose from the grave with an everlasting and living body which was one of the mysteries of God hidden from the beginning of time. Satan cares nothing about man, only his hatred for the man child of the woman and his hatred for the woman that brought the man child into this world.

4.) <u>This beast has seven heads</u>. The seven heads will be explained in chapter eighteen.

5.) <u>This beast has ten horns</u>. The ten horns will be explained in chapter eighteen.

6.) <u>This beast has seven crowns</u>. Daniel 7:7-8 **"After this I saw in the night visions, and behold a fourth beast, dreadful and terrible, and strong exceedingly; and it had great iron teeth: it devoured and brake in pieces, and stamped the residue with the feet of it: and it was diverse from all the beast that were before it; and it had ten horns. I considered the horns, and, behold, there came up among them another little horn, before whom there were three of the first horns plucked up by the roots: and, behold, in this horn were the eyes like the eyes of man, and a mouth speaking great things."** Revelation 13:1 **"And I stood upon the sand of the sea, and saw a beast rise up out of the sea, having seven heads and ten horns, and upon his horns ten crowns, and upon his heads the name of blasphemy."** They are the same beast, the one Daniel saw and the one John saw. This is explained in chapter seventeen.

Vs 4 **" And his tail drew the third part of the stars of heaven, and dist cast them to the earth: and the dragon stood before the woman which was ready to be delivered, for to devour her child as soon as it was born."**

This is the explanation of Revelation chapter six where the stars were cast unto the earth under the sixth seal. Satan's angels are called stars and are cast unto the earth. Under the fifth trumpet in chapter nine, Satan is cast unto the earth. This dragon stood before the woman ready to devour the child as soon as it was born. Satan knows that the child is the promised seed of the woman that God told Satan would crush his head and the seed of the woman will bruise his heal. Satan hates the woman for bringing the man child into this world. This verse gives us the reason why the great red dragon hates the woman.

THE THIRD CHARACTER- THE MAN CHILD

Vs 5   **"And she brought forth a man child, who was to rule all nations with a rod of iron: and her child was caught up unto God, and to his throne."**

David prophesied that God's Son will rule over Zion with a rod of iron in Psalm two. This man child is non other than Jesus Christ the very Son of God and he is caught up to heaven to his throne in heaven. Like the shepherds crook the rod of Jesus Christ is a comfort to those that follow the shepherd and is protection, but unto those that do not follow the shepherd, it is a terror and shall break them like a potters vessel into many pieces. Jesus stands at the door and knocks today and all those that open the door of their hearts, he will come in and save them, but at the end of the seven years of tribulation Jesus will rule with a rod of iron and break all those that have rejected him into pieces. Jesus is in heaven right now interceeding on the Christians behalf as our High Priest to the Father day and night. At the end of the tribulation period Jesus will return to this earth and rule and reign for a thousand years.

Vs 6 **"And the woman fled into the wilderness, where she hath a place prepared of God, that they should feed her there a thousand two hundred and threescore days."**

Because Satan and his angels are cast unto the earth, he is infuriated with the woman and will try to destroy every last Jew on this earth. Only by the intervention of God will the 144,000 Jews be saved and protected for the last forty two months of the tribulation period. God has a place prepared for them where He will feed them and protect them till the end of His judgement on those who have received the mark of the anti-christ and worship him as their god.

THE FOURTH CHARACTER- MICHAEL

Vs 7-8 **"And there was a war in heaven: Michael and his angels fought against the dragon; and the dragon fought and his angels, and prevailed not; neither was their place found any more in heaven."**

At some point during the seven years of tribulation all mankind will have made a decision whether to follow the anti-christ and receive his mark or to follow Jesus Christ and give their life as a testamony of their faith. All mankind

will either wear the mark of the beast or wear the seal of God around the middle

of the tribulation period. When the fate of all those on the earth is determined by

which seal they wear, then there will be no need for Satan to accuse the righteous

any longer in heaven. There will be a war in heaven where Satan and all his

angels will be cast out of heaven and into the earth. Satan and his angels have

their wings pulled off, so to speak, and made to dwell on the earth for the last

forty-two months of the tribulation. Satan is infuriated like a spoiled child and

goes on a killing rampage against the woman that brought the man child into this

world.

Vs 9 **"And the great dragon was cast out, that old serpent, called the Devil, and**

Satan, which deceiveth the whole world: he was cast out into the earth, and

his angels were cast out with him."

This is the explanation of the sixth seal and the fifth trumpet.

We are given five names for Satan:

1.) Great red dragon

2.) Old serphent

3.) Devil

4.) Satan

5.) Deceiver of the whole world

THE FIFTH CHARACTER- THE LAMB AND HIS BLOOD

Vs 10 **"And I heard a loud voice saying in heaven, Now is come salvation, and strength, and the kingdom of our God, and the power of his Christ: for the accuser of our brethren is cast down, which accused them before our God day and night."**

Satan has no more access to heaven to accuse the Christians. Christians fall into sin because we still live in this flesh that has inherited a sin nature from our earthly father Adam. The difference between the lost man and the saved man is that a saved man wants to serve Jesus as a spiritual man and the lost man wants to serve the flesh and satisfy the fleshly desires. It is like the cat and pig nature. You can wash a pig and put perfume on him and parade him up and down the church isles and he will look just like all the other Christians. But, when you turn a pig loose in the barn yard, he will find the first mud hole and bury up to his nose in the mud. It is his natural desire to get into the mud hole and stay there. The cat, on the other hand, will walk around the barn yard avoiding mud where he walks. When the cat does get mud on his feet, he will lick it off as soon as he is out of the mud. The cat's nature is like a Christian's will to serve Jesus Christ. He may get into sin, but he wants to get out of it and clean it out of his life. The pig's nature is like a lost man, he loves the mud and he loves sin and when he gets into it, he does not have the desire to get out of it.

Vs 11 "And they overcame him by the blood of the Lamb, and by the Word of their

testimony; and they loved not their lives unto the death."

There are three things a Christian has victory over Satan in this verse:

1.) A Christian overcomes Satan by the blood of the Lamb. When we are

washed in the blood of the Lamb of God, Satan may destroy the flesh, but

the soul and spirit of man is saved for eternity and can not be taken away.

Luke 10:27-30 **"My sheep hear my voice, and I know them, and they**

follow me: And I give unto them eternal life; and they shall never

perish, neither shall any man pluck them out of my hand. My Father,

which gave them me, is greater than all; and no man is able to pluck

them out of my Father's hand. I and my Father are one."

2.) A Christian overcomes Satan by the word of their testimony. Matthew

10:32-33 **"Whosoever therefore shall confess me before men, him will**

I confess also before my Father which is in heaven. But whosoever

shall deny me before men, him will I also deny before my Father

which is in heaven." Romans 10:9-13 **"That if thou shalt confess with**

thy mouth the Lord Jesus, and shalt believe in thine heart that God

hath raised him from the dead, thou shalt be saved. For with the heart

man believeth unto righteousness; and with the mouth confession is

made unto salvation. For the scripture saith, Whosoever believeth on him shall not be ashamed. For there is no difference between the Jew and the Greek: for the same Lord over all is rich unto all that call upon him. For whosoever shall call upon the name of the Lord shall be saved."

3.) A Christian during the tribulation will ultimately give his life as a testamony of his faith in Jesus Christ. Revelation 20:4 **"And I saw thrones, and they that sat upon them, and judgment was given unto them; and I saw the souls of them that were beheaded for the witness of Jesus, and for the Word of God, and which had not worshiped the beast, neither his image, neither had received his mark upon their foreheads, or in their hands; and they lived and reigned with Christ a thousand years."** We are living in the grace age, when we are not persecuted for our faith in Jesus Christ. What a testamony the tribulation saints will give for Jesus.

THE THIRD WOE

Vs 12 **"Therefore rejoice, ye heavens, and ye that dwell in them. Woe to the inhabiters of the earth and the sea, for the devil is come down unto you, having great wrath, because he knoweth that he hath but a short time."**

There is rejoicing in heaven because Satan has been cast unto the earth, but on the earth there will be the final vials or bowls of the wrath of God cast upon those who wear the mark of the beast. Satan is furrious because he has lost access to heaven and now dwells on the earth for a short time. Satan knows that he has almost forty-two months left before his end.

Vs 13 **"And when the dragon saw that he was cast unto the earth, he persecuted the woman which brought forth the man child."**

If the world thought Hitler was bad, they will see anti-Semitism at its worst. This time of the Jew's persecution is called "Jacobs troubles" in Jeremiah chapter thirty and thirty one. Jesus refered to this tim of persecution in Mathew chapter twenty four. All of Israel will be killed for their testimony and worshiping Jesus Christ, except for the 144,000 who have been sealed with the seal of God in their foreheads. The Jew would be totally anialated except for God's intervention in saving the 144,000. The anti-christ will make Hitler look like a school boy in comparison to his hatred for the Jew.

Vs 14 **"And to the woman were given two wings of a great eagle, that she might fly into the wilderness, into her place, where she is nourished for a time, and times, and half a time, from the face of the serpent."**

The time frame is given in this verse for the casting of Satan onto the earth and his persecuting the woman to the end of the tribulation period. A time is one year, times is two years and half a time is half a year which makes up forty-two months. The Woman represents the 144,000 Jews that have received the seal of God in their foreheads. John sees a great eagle helping the woman escape to the wilderness to what is called her place. This great eagle may represent the United States of America, that helps the 144,000 Jews escape to her place in the wilderness and feeds them for the forty-two months. The place that the woman flies to is called a wilderness. If it is the USA that the woman flies to, then it will be a wilderness. We know that under the six seals that have been opened, there will be a war on the earth and one third of the earth will be devestated by the plagues under the six seals. The United States is not mentioned in Revelation and may not be a great power in the world during this time. There may be some Jews in the United States that will help the 144,000 escape to this wilderness. With all the remaining bowls of the wrath of God to come upon the earth and the persuit of the anti-christ to destroy all the remaining Jews upon the earth, God is the one that protects the 144,000 Jews and feeds them for forty-two months.

Vs 15-16 **"And the serpent cast out of his mouth water as a flood after the woman, that he might cause her to be carried away of the flood. And the earth helped the woman, and the earth opened her mouth, and swallowed up the flood which the dragon cast out of his mouth."**

The water out of the mouth of the serpent represents an army. Isaiah 8:7-8 **Now therefore, behold, the Lord bringeth up upon them the waters of the river, strong and many, even the king of Assyria, and all his glory: and he shall come up over all his channels, and go over all his banks: And he shall pass through Judah; he shall overflow and go over, he shall reach even to the neck; and the stretching out of his wings shall fill the breath of thy land, O Immanuel."** This army invades Israel to destroy all men, women and children, but the flood or army does not catch the 144,000 Jews that have the seal of God in their foreheads. The earth opens up and swallows the flood or army sent by the serpent.

Vs 17 **"And the dragon was wroth with the woman, and went to make war with the remnant of her seed, which keep the commandments of God, and have the testimony of Jesus Christ."**

The dragon hates the Jew and now focusses his attention on all the remaining Jews in the world that have not received his mark and have not worshiped him as god. This is again the time of Jacob's troubles and the time Jesus tells about in Matthew chapter twenty four. All the Jews will be killed as their testimony of Jesus Christ as verse eleven so clearly states.

REVELATION CHAPTER 13

<u>THE SIXTH CHARACTER- THE BEAST OUT OF THE SEA</u>

Vs 1   **"And I stood upon the sand of the sea, and saw a beast rise up out of the sea, having seven heads and ten horns, and upon his horns ten crowns, and upon his heads the name of blasphemy."**

This beast out of the sea is a political beast. He is the anti-Christ that takes control of the entire world. He rises to power very quickly. John sees this beast with seven heads. Revelation 17:9 **"And here is the mind which hath wisdom. The seven heads are seven mountains, on which the woman sitteth."** The seven heads are seven mountains, which most Bible scholars agree as being that great city of Rome. The ten horns with ten crowns upon this beast head represent ten kingdoms that give him power. Revelation 17:12 **"And the ten horns which thou sawest are ten kings, which have received no kingdom as yet; but receive power as kings one hour with the beast."** The sea that John saw the beast rise up from represents many people and nations. Revelation 17:15 **"And he saith unto me, the waters which thou sawest, where the whore sitteth, are peoples, and multitudes, and nations, and tongues."** John sees the anti-Christ rise out of the sea of humanity to a position of great authority and power in that great city of Rome with the name of blasphemy on his seven heads.

Vs 2   **"And the beast which I saw was like unto a leopard, and his feet were as the feet of a bear, and his mouth as the mouth of a lion: and the dragon gave him his power, and his seat, and great authority."**

King Nebuchadnezzar had a dream and could not remember the dream. He called all his wise men, astrologers, magicians and soothsayers in to tell him the dream and interpret it to him. When they could not even tell him what he had dreamed, the king decreed that all the wise men including Daniel would be put to death. Daniel prayed and God revealed the dream and the interpretation to Daniel. Daniel 2:31-45 **"Thou, O king, sawest, and behold a great image. The great image, whose brightness was excellent, stood before thee; and the form thereof was terrible. This image's head was of fine gold, his breast and his arms of silver, his belly and his thighs of brass, his legs of iron, his feet part of iron and part of clay. Thou sawest till that a stone was cut out without hands, which smote the image upon his feet that were of iron and clay, and brake them to pieces. Then was the iron, the clay, the brass, the silver, and the gold, broken to pieces together, and became like chaff of the summer threshing floors; and the wind carried them away, that no place was found for them: and the stone that smote the image became a great mountain, and filled the whole earth. This is the dream; and we will tell interpretation thereof before the king. Thou, O king, art a king of kings: for the God of heaven hath given thee a kingdom, power, and strength, and glory. And** wheresoever the children of men dwell, the beast of the field and the fowls of the heaven hath he given into thine hand, and hath made thee ruler over them all. <u>Thou art this head of gold.</u> And after thee shall arise another kingdom inferior to thee, and another third kingdom of brass, which shall bear rule over all the earth. And the fourth kingdom shall be strong as iron: forasmuch as iron breaketh in pieces and subdueth all things: and as iron that breaketh all these, shall it break in pieces and bruise. And whereas thou sawest the feet and the toes, part of potters' clay, and part of iron, the kingdom shall be devided; but there shall be in it of the strength of the iron, forasmuch as thou sawest the iron mixed with miry clay. And as the toes of the feet were part of iron, and part of clay, so the kingdom shall be partly strong, and partly broken. And whereas thou sawest iron mixed with miry clay, they shall mingle themselves with the seed of men: but they shall not cleave one to another, even as iron is not mixed with clay. And in the days of these kings shall the God of heaven set up a kingdom, which shall never be destroyed: and the kingdom shall not be left to other people, but it shall break in pieces and consume all these kingdoms, and it shall stand for ever. Forasmuch as thou sawest that the stone was cut out of the mountain without hands, and that it brake in pieces the iron, the brass, the clay, the silver, and the gold; the great God hath made known to the king what shall come to pass hereafter: and the dream is certain, and the interpretation therof sure."

Daniel revealed the world kingdoms or powers that were to be till the end of time to King Nebuchadnezzar. The first world power was the Babylonian Empire under Nebuchadnezzar. This was the head of gold. The second world power would be the Media Persian Empire. This was the breast and arms of silver. Notice the two arms of silver and the two rulers. The third world power would be the Grecian Empire ruled by Alexander the Great. This was the bronze belly and thighs. After the death of Alexander the kingdom was divided between his four generals. The fourth world power would be the Roman Empire. This is the iron legs which later divided into the east and west empire. Notice the two legs which represent the divided empire. The last world empire will be the revival of the Roman Empire. This is the feet of iron and the ten toes of iron and miry clay. The final world power will be the kingdom of our Lord Jesus Christ as the stone that is cut out without hands and destroys the beast by smiting it on its feet and toes. The revival of the Roman Empire will be destroyed by the stone cut out without hands which is Jesus Christ.

The beast that John describes is a composite of the four beast that Daniel describes in Daniel chapter seven. The characteristics of the beast that John describes are similar to all the world empires of the past. The leopard represents the Grecian Empire, the feet of a bear represents the Media-Persian Empire and the mouth of a lion represents the Babylonian Empire. Great power was given to this beast like a combination of all the world powers before.

Vs 3   **"And I saw one of his heads as it were wounded to death; and his deadly wound was healed: and all the world wondered after the beast."**

There are three interpretations that may fit the explanation of this verse where one of the heads of the beast is wounded to death and his wound is healed:

1.) This beast may be the Roman Empire that has been wounded to death and is revived again to a world power. The total power that the Roman Empire had over the world as a dictator government will again be revived according to Daniel and to John's letter that we are studying. The only trouble with this interpretation is that this beast is referred to as a man all the way through this chapter. Although the Roman Empire will be revived, this may not be the interpretation of the deadly wound being healed.

2.) This beast may be a Roman Caesar who has ruled the Roman Empire before and is revived from the dead. This would require that the man was kept in a frozen state or something like science fiction movies, where the man is brought back to life. This is not likely, for Jesus would be the only person that could bring anyone back to life from the grave and a Roman Caesar would not be a likely person for Jesus to raise from the dead.

3.) We are told something about where this beast comes from. Revelation 17:7-8 **"And the angel said unto me, wherefore didst thou marvel? I will tell thee the mystery of the woman, and of the beast that carrieth her, which hath the seven heads and the ten horns. The beast that thou sawest was, and is not: and <u>shall ascend out of the bottomless pit,</u> and go into perdition: and they that dwell on the earth shall wonder, whose names were not written in the book of life from the foundation of the world, when they behold the beast that was, and is not, and yet is."** This beast was a man, but at the present time that John wrote the Revelation, was not alive and is yet to be alive again during the tribulation period. This beast is the anti-Christ and may very well be the son of Satan, born for the purpose of trying to imitate the Son of God.

a.) John 6:64-71 **"But there are some of you that believe not. For Jesus knew from the beginning who they were that believed not, and who should betray him. And he said, Therefore said I unto you, that no man can come unto me, except it were given unto him of my Father. From that time many of his disciples went back, and walked no more with him. Then said Jesus unto the twelve, Will ye also go away? Then Simon Peter answered him, Lord, to whom shall we go? Thou hast the words of eternal life. And we believe and are sure that thou art the Christ, the Son of the living God. Jesus answered them, <u>Have not I chosen you twelve, and one of you is a devil?</u> He spake of**

Judas Iscariot the son of Simon: for it was he it was that should betray him, being one of the twelve."

b.) John 17:8-12 "For I have given unto them the words which thou gavest me; and they have received them, and have known surely that I came out from thee, and they have believed that thou didst send me. I pray for them: I pray not for the world, but for them which thou hast given me; for they are thine. And all mine are thine, and thine are mine; and I am glorified in them. And now I am no more in the world, but these are in the world, and I come to thee. Holy Father, keep through thine own name those whom thou hast given me, that they may be one, as we are one. While I was with them in the world, I kept them in thy name; those that thou gavest me I have kept, and none of them is lost, but the son of perdition; that the scripture might be fulfilled." The first word "kept" has the meaning of pastoral regard and second word "kept" means guarded from external assaults.

c.) II Thessalonians 2:3 "Let no man deceive you by any means; for that day shall not come, except there come a falling away first, and that man of sin be revealed, the son of perdition; Who opposeth and exhalteth himself above all that is called God, or that is worshipped; so

that he as God sitteth in the temple of God, showing himself that he is

God."

Some how Judas Iscariot who was alive while Christ was on this earth and

was dead at the time of John's writing this passage, will come up out of the

bottomless pit to live again as the anti-Christ and the beast that rises out of the sea

during the tribulation period. Judas might be the son of Satan, to do Satan's

bidding in trying to destroy Jesus Christ as God's Son. Satan is an imitator, and

because God had a Son, Satan may have a son also. Judas was referred to as the

"son of perdition" by Jesus himself. Acts 1:18-20 **"Now this man purchased a**

field with the reward of iniquity; and falling headlong, he burst asunder in

the midst, and all his bowels gushed out. And it was known unto all the

dwellers at Jerusalem; inasmuch as the field is called in their proper tongue,

Aceldama, that is to say, the field of blood. For it is written in the book of

Psalms, Let his habitation be desolate, and let no man dwell therein: and, his

office let another take." Judas habitation may be in the bottomless pit which is

reserved for the fallen angels and is not occupied by any other man except the

anti-Christ and the false prophet during the thousand year reign of Christ on this

earth. In the last forty two months of the tribulation period, Judas or the anti-

Christ or the beast that rises up out of the sea will exalt himself to be worshipped

as God by all the world, except for the 144,000 Jews that have received the seal of

God in their foreheads. This is just speculation and the beast could be someone else.

Vs 4   **"And they worshipped the dragon which gave power unto the beast: and they worshipped the beast, saying, Who is like unto the beast? Who is able to make   war with him?"**

Satan is not opposed to religion, in fact he uses religion to exalt himself to this position where he is worshipped as god. When Jesus began his ministry and went into the desert, Satan tempted him three times. Satan's offer of giving the world to Jesus if he would only fall down and worship him, revealed his very desire to be God. There may be some that will say that Jesus was raised from the grave on the third day after the crucifixion and those who worship the beast will say that their god was raised from the dead also. Satan is an imitator of everything that God has done. Whether his deadly wound being healed is a great trick played upon the world or if it really happens, we do not know. The beast that came up out of the sea is worshipped as God by the whole world. If the world does not comply with his demands then he makes war with them and destroys them. The world fears the anti-Christ as well as worship him.

Vs 5　**"And there was given unto him a mouth speaking great things and blasphemies; and power was given unto him to continue forty and two months."**

"And there was given unto him" is mentioned two times in this verse and four more times in this chapter. Satan will never be able to say to God that he was never given his chance to be worshipped like God. He is given a mouth speaking great things. Satan was a liar from the beginning and he will lie to the world about the beast in order to get them to believe he is God. He was given power. There is no doubt that Satan has great power. Today the Holy Spirit prevents Satan from using his great power to lie and trick his way to being worshipped by the world as God. When the Holy Spirit is taken out of the way, then Satan will have unrestrained power. II Thessalonians 2:7 **"For the mystery of iniquity doth already work: only he who now letteth will let, until he be taken out of the way."** When the true church or believers in Jesus Christ is raptured out, the Holy Spirit is taken out with the church. The born again believer are the temple of the Holy Spirit at this present time. This is why the church is referred to as those who are born again. The Holy Spirit does not live in a building.

Vs 6　**"And he opened his mouth in blasphemy against God, to blaspheme his name, and his tabernacle, and them that dwell in heaven."**

I always have heard that the Bible teaches us if we do not have anything good to say about someone, just say nothing. Well, Satan might be just the opposite. He blasphemes God, the Holy Spirit, Jesus, the Word of God, the church and the Jews. It seems funny that those who reject Jesus Christ and say there is no God in heaven still curse God and blaspheme his Word.

Vs 7 **"And it was given unto him to make war with the saints, and to overcome them: and power was given him over all kindreds, and tongues, and nations."**

"And it was given unto him" again to make war on all those who worship the true and living Christ. The beast declares open season to kill all those that worship the true Christ. The Christians have never seen the time in history that will compare to this time of persecution.

Vs 8 **"And all that dwell upon the earth shall worship him, whose names are not written in the book of life of the Lamb slain from the foundation of the world."**

John clarifies this statement to point out who worships the beast. The 144,000 Jews that have received the seal of God in their forehead do not worship the beast, but worship God and Jesus Christ. Their names are written in the Lambs book of life.

Vs 9-10 **"If any man have an ear, let him hear. He that leadeth into captivity shall go into captivity: he that killeth with the sword must be killed with the sword. Here is the patience and the faith of the saints."**

This is a warning to those who have not worshipped the beast. He that leads them into captivity will ultimately be led into captivity themselves. Those men who follow the anti-Christ and kill the saints that believe in Jesus Christ, will ultimately be killed with the sword. It is futile for the saints to fight against the anti-Christ and they are urged to be patient waiting for the return of Christ to destroy them that kill the saints of God.

THE SEVENTH CHARACTER- THE BEAST OUT OF THE EARTH

Vs 11 **"And I beheld another beast coming up out of the earth; and he had two horns like a lamb, and spake as a dragon."**

This beast is called the false prophet and is the religious beast. We see the trinity of Satan. Satan imitates God, the beast out of the sea imitates Christ and the beast out of the earth imitates the Holy Spirit. This beast that rises up out of the earth is the power behind Satan and the anti-Christ. This beast is not omnipresent, being everywhere at the same time as the Holy Spirit. John sees this beast come up out of the earth. This may represent that he comes from Hell, which is located at the center of the earth. Deuteronomy 32:22 **"For a fire is kindled in mine anger, and shall burn unto the lowest hell, and shall consume the earth with her increase, and set on fire the foundations of the mountains."** This beast had two horns like a lamb. He may look like a lamb to the world, being very holy and the leader of religion, but he spoke as a dragon. This beast is a religious beast and causes the world to worship the first beast as God.

Vs 12 **"And he exerciseth all the power of the first beast before him, and causeth the earth and them which dwell therein to worship the first beast, whose deadly wound was healed."**

I John 4:1-3 **"Beloved, believe not every spirit, but try the spirits whether they are of God: because many false prophets are gone out into the world. Hereby know ye the Spirit of God: Every spirit that confesseth that Jesus Christ is come in the flesh is of God: And every spirit that confesseth not that Jesus Christ is come in the flesh is not of God: and this is the spirit of anti-Christ, whereof ye have heard that it should come; and even now already is it in the world."** John warned the church to be aware of those spiritual leaders that magnify anything else but that Jesus Christ has come in the flesh and is the Son of God. If the spiritual leaders magnify the mother of Jesus or their membership in the church or their being baptized or being forgiven by a priest or keeping the law or anything other than Jesus Christ as God's Son and him crucified for the sins of the world, then John calls him the spirit of anti-Christ. This false prophet that rises up out of the earth not only rejects Jesus Christ but magnifies the first beast that came up out of the sea as God to be worshipped by the whole world. This false prophet is the spiritual leader of the apostate church during the tribulation period. The woman that rides the scarlet colored beast in chapter seventeen is the apostate church that gives great power to the beast and causes the world to worship the beast. Revelation 17:9 **"Here is the mind which hath wisdom, the seven heads are seven mountains, on which the woman sitteth."** Revelation 17:18 **"And the woman which thou sawest is that great city, which reigneth over the kings of the earth."** This great city is Rome which sits on seven mountains is the woman John saw riding on the scarlet colored beast that seven heads and ten horns.

Vs 13 **"And he doeth great wonders, so that he maketh fire come down from heaven on the earth in sight of men."**

This false prophet has power from Satan to do great wonders. The men on the earth have forgotten the two witnesses that preached for the first forty two months and their miracles and their message of Jesus Christ as God's Son. Satan does have great power as seen by Pharaoh's magicians when Moses laid his staff down at Pharaoh's feet. Moses's staff turned into a snake and the magicians staffs became snakes. The thing Pharaoh refussed to see was that God's power was greater than Satan's power and Moses's staff swallowed up the magician's staffs. Satan has power that the men on the earth will believe over the power of the two witnesses of God.

Vs 14 **"And deceived them that dwell on the earth by means of those miracles which he had power to do in the sight of the beast; saying to them that dwell on the earth, that they should make an image to the beast, which had the wound by a sword, and did live."**

The Jews will see this as a direct violation of the word of God to make a graven image to be worshipped as God. This may be the very day that the nation of Israel rejects the first beast that rises up out of the sea as the messiah that they looked for and turn to the messiah preached by the two witnesses that rise up from the dead in the streets of Jerusalem and go into heaven in a cloud. These two events may happen in the same day. Those who have rejected the message of the two witnesses believe the lies and the miracles of the false prophet and worship the image of the first beast that had a wound by a sword and did live.

Vs 15 **"And he had power to give life unto the image of the beast, that the image of the beast should both speak, and cause that as many as would not worship the image of the beast should be killed."**

The religious beast joins the political beast and the power of the false prophet is given to the anti-Christ. We know that this power is coming from Satan and all men on the earth are now forced to make a decision, whether to worship the image of the anti-Christ or believe in Jesus Christ and be killed for their testimony.

Vs 16-17 **"And he causeth all, both small and great, rich and poor, free and bond, to receive a mark in their right hand, or their foreheads: And that no man might buy or sell, save he that had the mark, or name of the beast, or the number of his name."**

The false prophet causes the whole world to make a decision to worship the image of the anti-Christ and receive his mark in their right hand or their forehead or be killed. There will be no straddling the fence in this decision, a man cannot receive the mark to stay alive and still believe in Jesus Christ. Revelation 14:9-10 **"And the third angel followed them. saying with a loud voice, if any man worship the beast and his image, and receive his mark in his forehead, or his hand, the same shall drink of the wine of the wrath of God,**

which is poured out without mixture into the cup of his indignation; and he
shall be tormented with fire and brimstone in the presence of the holy angels,
and in the presence of the Lamb." All men during the tribulation period will be
forced to make a decision to live and continue to buy and sell or to die for their
belief in Jesus Christ.

Vs 18 **"Here is wisdom. Let him that hath understanding count the number of a
man; and his number is six hundred threescore and six."**

The mark of the beast is the number is 666. The worlds system for buying
and selling is already set up for the number of the beast. This number may very
well be the bar code that is used to purchase and record every product in the
world, what it is, what size, what manufacturer, what plant, where it is purchased,
everything. There are spaces in the bar code reserved for identification purposes
right now. If the present day bar code is not used, it can be changed by simply
reprogramming all the scanners to where only the false prophet has access to
change it. There already exist a record of every person in the United States, their
address, age, employer, salary, children, make and model car, your bank account,
what you owe, what you have, and even things you do not know about yourself. It
is all set up just waiting for one person to join all the wires to one master
computer where everything will be controlled by one man.

REVELATION CHAPTER 14

John sees the end of the tribulation period with the Lamb standing on Mount Zion, which is the holy city Jerusalem with the 144,000 Jews. John continues the break from chapter twelve to chapter nineteen and verse eleven with explanations or what may be called flashbacks to events already covered under the seven sealed scroll. This chapter will picture the Lamb with the 144,000 Jews that wear the seal of God in their foreheads, the proclamation of the everlasting gospel, the pronouncement of judgment on Babylon, the pronouncement of judgment on those who have received the mark of the beast, the praise of those who die for their testimony of Jesus Christ during the tribulation and the preview of the battle of Armageddon.

Vs 1   **"And I looked, and, lo, a Lamb stood on Mount Zion, and with him a hundred forty and four thousand, having his Father's name written in their foreheads."**

This is the Son of God, the Lamb of God, Jesus Christ our Lord and Savior. This is a flash forward to the end event of the tribulation when Jesus Christ comes back to the earth. At the end of the tribulation there will be no flesh left alive on this earth except for these 144,000 Jews that have the seal of God in their foreheads. Jesus will return to this earth at Mount Zion in Jerusalem.

Vs 2-3 **"And I heard a voice from heaven, as the voice of many waters, and as the voice of a great thunder: and I heard the voice of harpers harping with their harps: And they sung as it were a new song before the throne, and before the four beast, and the elders: and no man could learn that song but the hundred and forty and four thousand, which were redeemed from the earth."**

The saints in heaven can not learn this new song that heavens choir is singing and playing on harps, but the 144,000 on the earth hear this song and they know the tune and the song. The churches on this earth today that do have music in their worship service will have to learn a lot of new tunes in heaven, but this is one that none of the saints in heaven can learn.

Vs 4 **"These are they which were not defiled with women; for they are virgins. These are they which follow the Lamb whithersoever he goeth. These were redeemed from among men, being the first fruits of God and to the Lamb."**

Revelation 7:4 **"And I heard the number of them which were sealed: and there were sealed a hundred and forty and four thousand of all the tribes of the children of Israel."** These may be actually children that are sealed with the seal of God. We are told they are virgins. When Jesus comes back to this earth, they follow him where ever he goes, like children. They were redeemed

from among men as the first born of God and the Lamb to repopulate the entire
earth for a thousand years.

Vs 5 **"And in their mouth was found no guile: for they are without fault before the
throne of God."**

They did not worship the anti-Christ and did no believe the lies of the
false prophet, they were innocent like little children. They may be children
literally, that are above the age of accountability. We know that in the rapture,
Jesus will come and take out all the righteous saints and those that have not
reached the age of accountability. These children that have not reached an age
where they know right and wrong will be taken out of this world with the saints of
God. What age these children are may vary from child to child and we are not
told in scripture. Matthew 19:14 **"But Jesus said, Suffer the little children,
and forbid them not, to come unto me: for of such is the kingdom of heaven."**
At the rapture there will be a large number of children that will be taken out of
this world before the judgment of God falls upon this earth during the tribulation
period. The tribulation will be so terrible that God may not allow children to
even be born during this time.

Vs 6 **"And I saw another angel fly in the midst of heaven, having the everlasting
gospel to preach unto them that dwell on the earth, and to every nation, and
kindred, and tongue, and people."**

There will be parade of "another angels" in this chapter with six angels communicating a message to the earth from heaven. For the first forty-two months the two witnesses preach the gospel message to those on the earth. During the last forty-two months God uses angels to carry his message to those on the earth. No man will be able to stand against the anti-Christ for the last forty-two months.

Vs 7 **"Saying with a loud voice, Fear God, and give glory to him; for the hour of his judgment is come: and worship him that made heaven, and earth, and the sea, and the foundations of waters."**

The gospel message goes out to all the earth, just in case there is someone in the darkest jungles on the earth that has not heard the message of Jesus Christ and him crucified for the sins of the world. II Corinthians 15:1-4 **"Moreover, brethren, I declare unto the gospel which I preached unto you, which also ye have received, and wherein ye stand; By which also ye are saved, if ye keep in memory what I preached unto you, unless ye have believed in vain. For I delivered unto you first of all that which I also received, how that Christ died for our sins according to the scriptures; and that he was buried, and that he rose again on the third day according to the scriptures."** This message is will cause fear to those who have received the mark of the beast because of the judgment of God that is coming upon the earth.

Vs 8   **"And there followed another angel, saying, Babylon is fallen, is fallen, that great city, because she made all nations drink of the wine of the wrath of her fornication."**

Isaiah chapter thirteen tells of the destruction of Babylon which shall never be dwelt by man again. The description of the destruction of religious Babylon and commercial Babylon will be covered in chapters seventeen and eighteen.

Vs 9-10   **"And the third angel followed them, saying with a loud voice, if any man worship the beast and his image, and receive his mark in his forehead, or in his hand, the same shall drink of the wine of the wrath of God, which is poured out without mixture into the cup of his indignation; and he shall be tormented with fire and brimstone in the presence of the holy angels, and in the presence of the Lamb."**

All mankind will make a choice to accept the mark of the beast or be killed. They have been warned by the two witnesses for forty-two months and here they are warned by an angel with a loud voice. When they stand before

Christ at the white throne judgment to give account of their sins and deeds on this earth, they cannot say that they did not know that if they received the mark of the beast that they were condemned to hell already. These angels messages are for the whole world to hear and just in case someone has not heard, they are told again that if they receive the mark of the beast they will be cast into the lake of fire called GEHENNA. The strange thing is that the majority of mankind will receive the mark of the beast anyway. The angels and Jesus Christ can look into GEHENNA and see their torment at any time but the saints of God are not able to see their torment. Many of our loved ones will be there and I am glad that we are not able to see their torment. Luke chapter sixteen describes the temporary hell called Hades. When a lost man dies today, he goes to Hades to be tormented in the flames there until he is brought out at the end of the thousand year reign of Christ on this earth. There will be a resurrection of the dead and every person that does not have his name recorded in the Lambs book of life will stand before the great white throne judgment and then be cast into GEHENNA for eternity. We will cover this in chapter twenty.

Vs 11 **"And the smoke of their torment ascendeth up for ever and ever: and they have no rest day or night, who worship the beast and his image, and whosoever receiveth the mark of his name."**

John jumps all the way to the end of the thousand year reign to give us a glimpse of what is in store for those who receive the mark of the beast in their right hand or in their forehead. When they are cast into the lake of fire or GEHENNA, the smoke of their torment is for eternity. There will be levels of punishment in GEHENNA. Men like Hitler must expect to be cast into the lower parts of GEHENNA where the darkness and the flames will be the hottest. Satan, the anti-Christ and the false prophet will obviously be at the very bottom.

Vs 12-13 **"Here is the patience of the saints: here are they that keep the commandments of God, and the faith of Jesus. And I heard a voice from heaven saying unto me, Write, blessed are the dead which die in the Lord from henceforth: Yea, saith the Spirit, that they may rest from their labors; and their works do follow them."**

There is praise from heaven for those that will die for their testimony for Jesus Christ from the middle of the tribulation till the end. The anti-Christ will persecute and kill all who do not receive his mark and have the testimony of Jesus Christ. It will be better to die for the Lord Jesus Christ, than to suffer eternal damnation in GEHENNA. After being killed for their testimony, they will be able to rest in heaven till the end of the tribulation period when they will receive a resurrected body just like those who were in the rapture at the beginning of the tribulation.

Vs 14 "And I looked, and behold a white cloud, and upon the cloud on sat like unto the Son of man, having on his head a golden crown, and in his hand a sharp sickle."

John flashes forward to the end of the tribulation period with the battle of Armageddon, beginning in chapter nineteen and verse eleven. The forces of the anti-Christ gather to destroy the remaining 144,000 Jews that are left on the earth, having killed all the other Jews on the earth. The comparison of this battle is like a man with a sharp sickle harvesting the grapes for the winepress. Acts 1:8-11 **"But ye shall receive power, after that the Holy Ghost is come upon you: and ye shall be witnesses unto me both in Jerusalem, and in all Judea, and Samaria, and unto the uttermost pert of the earth. And when he had spoken these things, while they beheld, he was taken up; and a cloud received him out of their sight. And while they looked steadfastly toward heaven as he went up, two men stood by them in white apparel; Which also said, Ye men of Galilee, why stand ye gazing up into heaven? This same Jesus, which is taken up from you into heaven, shall so come in like manner as ye have seen him go into heaven."** Jesus will return in a cloud back to this earth to set up his kingdom for a thousand years. John sees a golden crown on his head as he returns. This is the King of Kings and Lord of Lords that is returning and not the Lamb of God when he was born on this earth, and not the deliverer to rapture his saints at the beginning of the tribulation. He has a sickle in his hand which is a picture of his judgment on those that have rejected him as their Lord and Savior. Revelation 1:7 **"Behold, he cometh with clouds; and every eye shall see him, and they also which pierced him: and all kindreds of the earth shall wail because of him, Even so, Amen."**

Vs 15 **"And another angel came out of the temple, crying with a loud voice to him that sat on the cloud, Thrust in thy sickle, and reap: for the time has come for thee to reap; for the harvest of the earth is ripe."**

"Another angel" is sent from the temple from God telling Jesus it is time to reap the earth for the harvest is ripe. Everything operates on God's timetable. God is precise in everything he does. The seven years or eighty-four months are up and it is time to harvest the earth.

Vs 16 **"And he that sat on the cloud thrust in his sickle on the earth; and the earth was reaped."**

It is futile for Satan, the anti-Christ, the false prophet and those who wear the mark of the beast to battle against Jesus Christ. They are all cut down with a single swipe of the sickle. Matthew 13:36-43 **"Then Jesus sent the multitude away, and went into the house: and his disciples came unto him, saying,**

Declare unto us the parable of the tares of the field. **He answered and said unto them, He that soweth the good seed is the Son of man; the field is the world; the good seed are the children of the kingdom; but the tares are the children of the wicked one; the enemy that sowed them is the devil; the harvest is the end of the world; and the reapers are the angels. As therefore the tares are gathered and burned in the fire; so shall it be in the end of this world. The Son of man shall send forth his angels, and gather out of his kingdom all things that offend, and them which do iniquity; and shall cast them into a furnace of fire: there shall be wailing and gnashing of teeth. Then shall the righteous shine forth as the sun in the kingdom of their Father. Who hath ears to hear, let him hear."** We do not harvest the seeds, but we plant the seeds of the gospel and they either take root or they die, as Matthew chapter thirteen tells us.

Vs 17-18 **"And another angel came out of the temple which is in heaven, he also having a sharp sickle. And another angel came out from the altar, which had power over fire; and cried with a loud cry to him that had the sharp sickle, saying, Thrust in thy sharp sickle, and gather the clusters of the vine of the earth; for her grapes are fully ripe."**

"Another angel" again comes out of heaven with a sharp sickle and is commanded by "another angel" to gather the clusters on the vine of the earth.

The angle from under the altar which has power over fire represents the judgment fire of God upon his altar that requires blood to appease his anger and judgment. These men on the earth do not have the atoning blood of Jesus on them, so their blood is required to satisfy the wrath of God. Notice that the grapes are ripe and they are ready to burst when they are gathered.

Vs 19-20 **"And the angel thrust in his sickle into the earth, and gathered the vine of the earth, and cast it into the great winepress of the wrath of God. And the winepress was trodden without the city, and the blood came out of the winepress, even unto the horses bridles, by the space of a thousand and six hundred furlongs."**

Matthew 26:52 **"for all they that take the sword shall perish with the sword."** The army of the anti-Christ tries to battle with Jesus with their sword and by the sword they perish. This angel gathers the clusters of grapes or the armies of the anti-Christ into the valley of Megeddo where they are trodden under the foot of Jesus Christ. This is covered in chapter nineteen. The blood of the armies runs for a length of two hundred miles in the valley of Megaddo to a depth or the horses bridles. Revelation 16:16 **"And he gathered them together into a place called in the Hebrew tongue Armageddon."** Joel chapter three tells of this great battle. Isaiah 63:1-6 **"Who is this that cometh from Edom, with dyed garments from Bozrah? This that is glorious in his apparel,** traveling in the greatness of his strength? <u>I that speak in righteousness, mighty to save.</u> Wherefore art thou red in thine apparel, and thy garments like him that treadeth in the winefat? I have trodden the winepress alone; and of the people there was none with me: for I will tread them in mine anger, and trample them in my fury; and their blood shall be sprinkled upon my garments, and I will stain all my raiment. For the day of vengeance is in mine   heart, and the year of my redeemed is come. And I looked, and there was none to help; and I wondered that there was none to uphold: therefore mine own arm brought salvation unto me; and my fury, it upheld me. And I will tread down the people in mine anger, and make them drunk in my fury, and I will bring down their strength to the earth." The army of the anti-Christ has shed the innocent blood of all those who refused to worship the beast and receive his mark, and now their blood is required to be shed like a ripe grape that is stomped on in the winepress. How shall we escape if we neglect the great salvation provided by our Lord Jesus Christ.

REVELATION CHAPTER 15

John explains some of the details of what he has already seen in the opening of the seven sealed scroll. He flashes back to opening of the seventh seal where he has already described the seven angels with the seven trumpet judgments. Under the seventh angel with his trumpet there are seven vials or bowl judgments that happen very quickly just before the Lord of Lord and King of Kings returns to the earth in a cloud.

Vs 1 **"And I saw another sign in heaven, great and marvelous, seven angels having the seven last plagues; for in them is filled up the wrath of God."**

The scene switches back to heaven and John sees the seven last plagues on the inhabitants on the earth that are filled to the top with the wrath of God. John saw another sign in heaven which connects back with the sign in heaven in chapter twelve and thirteen where he saw the seven characters. This is a continuation of another sign in heaven.

Vs 2 **"And I saw as it were a sea of glass mingled with fire: and them that had gotten the victory over the beast, and over his image, and over his mark, and over the number of his name, stand on the sea of glass, having the harps of God."**

The sea of glass is the same as Revelation 4:6 explanation and now it is mingled with fire. The streets of heaven are pure gold as clear glass and the picture around the throne with the wrath of God being poured out on the inhabitants on the earth is like fire on the sea of glass. The souls of tribulation saints that have been killed for their testimony of Jesus Christ stand on the sea of glass around the throne of God. Revelation 6:10-11 **"And they cried with a loud voice, saying, How long, O Lord, holy and true, dost thou not judge and avenge our blood on them that dwell on the earth? And white robes were given unto every one of them; and it was said unto them, that they should rest yet for a little season, until their fellow servants also and their brethren, that should be killed as they were, should be fulfilled."** Those fellow servants have been killed now and their cry for Jesus Christ to avenge their blood is about to take place.

Vs 3-4   **"And they sing the song of Moses the servant of God, and the song of the Lamb, saying, Great and marvelous are thy works, Lord God Almighty; Just and true are thy ways, thou King of saints. Who shall not fear thee, O Lord, and glorify thy name? For thou only art holy: For all nations shall come and worship before thee; for thy judgments are made manifest."**

The song of Moses is sung in Exodus chapter fifteen and the song of the Lamb is sung in Revelation chapter five. The time of fulfillment of these songs has come.

Vs 5-6   **"And after that I looked, and, behold, the temple of the tabernacle of the testimony in heaven was opened. And the seven angels came out of the temple, having the seven plagues, clothed in pure and white linen, and having their breast girded with golden girdles."**

The holy of holies in the temple where the ark of the covenant is kept is opened. The plans for the ark and the temple on the earth that were given to Moses were a copy of the original in heaven. Exodus 25:40 **"And look that thou make them after their pattern, which was showed thee in the mount."** These angels come out of the holy of holies and have a priestly garment different from the other angels. When John first saw Jesus standing in the middle of the seven candlesticks, he had on a priestly garment also. Revelation 1:13 **"And in the midst of the seven candlesticks one like unto the Son of man, clothed with a garment down to the foot, and girt about the paps with a golden girdle."** The holy of holies is where the blood sacrifice was taken in by the high priest to be offered to satisfy the wrath of God for his judgment on the sins of the people. There is no blood sacrifice for those on the earth that wear the mark of the beast and God's judgment must fall on them. These angels minister the wrath of God upon those that do not have the blood of the Lamb of God to forgive them of their sins.

Vs 7   **"And one of the four beast gave unto the seven angels seven golden vials full of the wrath of God, who liveth for ever and ever."**

These angels do not take bowls of blood into the altar but bring bowls of the wrath of God out to cast onto those that dwell on the earth. The first three bowls of the wrath of God deal with blood.

Vs 8   **"And the temple was filled with smoke from the glory of God, and from his power; and no man was able to enter into the temple, till the seven plagues of the seven angels were fulfilled."**

Exodus 40:34-35 **"Then a cloud covered the tent of the congregation, and the glory of the Lord filled the tabernacle. And Moses was not able to enter into the tent of the congregation, because the cloud abode thereon, and the glory of the Lord filled the tabernacle."** I Kings 8:10-11 **"And it came to pass, when the priest were come out of the holy place, that the cloud filled the house of the Lord. So that the priest could not stand to minister because of the cloud: for the glory of the Lord had filled the house of the Lord."** When the tabernacle on the earth was built the Lord filled the holy of holies with his glory and no man was able to enter. God's wrath now fills the tabernacle in heaven and no man is able to enter.

REVELATION CHAPTER 16

The seven angels are given seven vials or bowls filled with the wrath of God and in this chapter John will describe what happens at the very close of the tribulation period. These judgments will come very quickly with one angel after another pouring their bowls upon those who wear the mark of the beast on the earth.

Vs 1   **"And I heard a great voice out of the temple saying to the seven angels, Go your ways, and pour out the vials of the wrath of God upon the earth."**

We have all heard a great deal about the love of God, but this chapter is all about the wrath of God upon those who reject the Lord Jesus Christ as their Lord and Savior. This voice is a great voice that commands the angels to go your way and pour out your bowls.

Vs 2   **"And the first went, and poured out his vial upon the earth; and there fell a noisome and grievous sore upon the men which had the mark of the beast, and upon them which worshipped his image."**

These judgments do not fall on the 144,000 Jews that are sealed with the seal of God. This judgment is against men's blood and causes grievous sores to come upon all who wear the mark of the beast.

Vs 3   **"And the second angel poured out his vial upon the sea; and it became as the blood of a dead man; and every living soul died in the sea."**

Under the second trumpet one third of the sea was turned to blood, but here all the seas become as the blood of a dead man. The blood is the life of the body and a dead mans blood has no life in it. There is no life in the sea at all and all that is in the sea will die.

Vs 4   **"And the third angel poured out his vial upon the rivers and the fountains of waters; and they became blood."**

Under the third trumpet one third of the fresh water was turned to blood, but here all the rivers and the water wells were turned to blood. The men on the earth have no fresh water to drink at all. We take water for granted today and our water is becoming more polluted every day. This will continue to happen even in this present time on the earth if man does not stop polluting and letting the fresh water slowly die to the point it will not support life.

Vs 5-6   **"And I heard the angel of the waters say, thou art righteous, O Lord, which art, and wast, and shall be, because thou has judged thus. For they have shed the blood of saints and prophets, and thou hast given them blood to drink; for they are worthy."**

These first three judgments may be the direct answer to the prayers of those saints that were under the altar and cried out for vengeance on those men on the earth that shed their blood and killed them for their testimony of Jesus Christ. The men on the earth were so blood thirsty in killing the saints and the Jews that they are worthy to be given blood to drink.

Vs 7   **"And I heard another out of the altar say, Even so, Lord God Almighty, true and righteous are thy judgments."**

Vs 8-9   **"And the fourth angel poured out his vial upon the sun; and power was given unto him to scorch men with fire, and men were scorched with great heat, and blasphemed the name of God, which hath power over these plagues: and they repented not to give him glory."**

All through the Old Testament this time is mentioned when men will be scorched with great heat. Deuteronomy 32:24; Isiah 24:6; Isiah 42:25; Malichi 4:1 are just a few. Matthew 24:22 **"And except those days should be shortened, there should no flesh be saved: but for the elect's sake those days shall be shortened."** Even the 144,000 will feel the heat turned up on this earth, and all of nature will suffer also. The wild life and green things will turn brown and begin to die from the lack of water and the great heat. This all happens right at the end of the tribulation period. Psalm 121 **"I will lift up mine eyes unto the hills, from whence commeth my help. My help commeth from the Lord, which made heaven and earth. He will not suffer thy foot to be moved: He that keepeth thee will not slumber. The Lord is thy keeper: The Lord is thy shade upon thy right hand. The sun shall not smite thee by the day, nor the moon by night. The Lord shall preserve thee from all evil: He shall preserve thy soul. The Lord shall preserve thy goings out and thy coming in from this time forth, and even for evermore."** The Lord Jesus Christ protects the 144,000 during this time of all the plagues on the earth.

Vs 10-11 **"And the fifth angel poured out his vial upon the seat of the beast; and his kingdom was full of darkness; and they gnawed their tongues for the pain, and blasphemed the God of heaven because of their pains and their sores, and repented not of their deeds."**

The seat of the beast starts out in Rome and may be the place where this angel pours out his bowl of judgment. The heat is turned up but the lights are turned off in his kingdom. Men do not have water and they are full of sores and their tongues are swollen. They gnawed their tongues due to the great pain they have to endure, but they do not repent of their evil deeds.

Vs 12 **"And the sixth angel poured out his vial upon the great river Euphrates; and the water thereof was dried up, that the way of the kings of the east might be prepared."**

God makes it easy for the armies of the east to make their way to the valley of Megeddo. With the millions that are in China, it is easy to see how the blood of the army will run for two hundred miles to the depth of the horses bridles in the battle of Armageddon.

Vs 13-14 **"And I saw three unclean spirits like frogs come out of the mouth of the dragon, and out of the mouth of the beast, and out of the mouth of the false prophet. For they are the spirits of devils, working miracles, which go forth unto the kings of the earth and of the whole world, to gather them to the battle of that great day of God Almighty."**

We see the trinity of Satan with the anti-Christ and the false prophet. Matthew 24:24 **"For there shall arise false Christ, and false prophets, and shall show great signs and wonders; insomuch that, if it were possible, they shall deceive the very elect."** The trinity of Satan uses every power they have to get the whole world to send their armies to battle in Israel. God is a trinity and Satan has imitated the trinity of God. There is God the Father, God the Son and God the Holy Spirit. There is Satan the Devil, Satan the anti-Christ as the son and

Satan the false prophet as the power of Satan. Man is a trinity also, there is man's soul, there is man's body and man's spirit.

Vs 15 **"Behold, I come as a thief. Blessed is he that watcheth, and keepeth his garments, lest he walk naked, and they see his shame."**

I Thessalonians 5:4 **"But ye, brethren, are not in darkness, that that day should overtake you as a thief."** Christ will not come as a thief for his true church when he raptures his bride out of this earth at the beginning of the tribulation period. The letter to the seventh church is the apostate church that will go into the tribulation period as the last church age. This church has shut the door and Christ is standing on the outside knocking for those on the inside to open the door. They have locked the door and Christ will come into them as a thief and they never expect him to get in. The apostate church believes that the anti-Christ is their God and will protect them. They have swallowed his lies, hook, line and sinker. They are not looking for the true Son of God, Jesus Christ to come back to this earth to usher in the thousand year reign on this earth. They may believe that they are already in the kingdom reign with the anti-Christ as their God.

Vs 16 **"And he gathered them together into a place called in the Hebrew tongue Armageddon."**

In the original text, this place is called "Har- Megeddon", which means mount of slaughter. This great army of the world will gather around this valley where God has selected the place they will ultimately meet their destruction.

Vs 17-18 **"And the seventh angel poured out his vial into the air; and there came a great voice out of the temple in heaven, from the throne, saying, it is done. And there were voices, and thunders, and lightning's; and there was a great earthquake, such as was not since men were upon the earth, so mighty an earthquake, and so great."**

This great voice from the temple in heaven saying "It is done" is much like the final words of Jesus on the cross "It is finished." The work of salvation was finished when Jesus died on the cross of Calvary. The work of Satan on this earth for damnation and the destruction of mankind is done. Man's time is up for rejecting the very work of Jesus on the cross of Calvary and rejecting the blood of Jesus which was shed for their sins. The day of man is over and now it is time for the day of our Lord upon this earth. This earthquake is similar to the seventh trumpet judgment with a great earthquake and great hail on this earth.

Vs 19-21 **"And the great city was divided into three parts, and the cities of the nations fell: and great Babylon came in remembrance before God, to give unto her the cup of the wine of the fierceness of his wrath. And every island** fled away, and the mountains were not found. And there fell upon men a great hail out of heaven, every stone about the weight of a tallent: and men blasphemed God because of the plague of the hail; for the plague thereof was exceeding great."

This description under the seventh bowl judgment is similar to the seventh trumpet. Revelation 11:19 "And the temple of God was opened in heaven, and there was seen in his temple the ark of his testament: and there were lightning's, and voices, and thundering, and an earthquake, and great hail." This is where John began the break in chapter twelve and is explaining things that have happened under the opening of the seven sealed scroll. John may see all the bowl judgments happening very quickly at the seventh trumpet and now the seventh bowl judgment is the same as the seventh trumpet judgment. Under the seventh bowl judgment we see great earthquakes on the earth as never seen since man was on the earth. This could support the gap theory between Genesis chapter one and verse one with an earlier earth that God destroyed and in verse two it lay dormant under the waters. Genesis 1:1-2 "In the beginning God created the heaven and the earth. And the earth was without form, and void; And darkness was upon the face of the deep. And the Spirit of God moved upon the face of the waters." There were earthquakes between these two verses in Genesis. What happened to cause the earth to be without form and void with a flood over the earth, we do not know. God die promise to Noah, that he would not destroy the earth with a flood again, implying that it was destroyed by a flood before. This earth was populated with gentle roaming giant creatures at one time and it may have been destroyed by Satan and his fallen angels, when Satan rebelled against God and were cast out of heaven onto the earth where he destroyed the earth. This could explain where the dinosaurs came from and the earth being millions of years old. According to the Bible, the presence of man on this earth has only been about six thousand years. This earth will be destroyed by God at the end of the tribulation period. All the islands will disappear, all the mountains will fall flat, all the cities of the world will fall and great hail shall beat the earth. There will be great hail with each stone weighing about a talent or about 116 pounds. This earth will be shaken and beaten down to remove the presence of all men on this earth.

MOORE ABOUT REVELATION

REVELATION CHAPTER 17

John continues the break from chapter twelve to chapter nineteen where he describes things that have already happened under the seven seals that have already been opened. Chapter seventeen and eighteen reveals the judgment of God on the religious Babylon and the commercial Babylon. In chapter seventeen John describes the judgment of God on the religious Babylon with a picture of a great whore that rides on the back of a scarlet colored beast. The whore is a picture of the apostate church that was described in the letter to the church at Laodicea in chapter three. This harlot is controlling the scarlet colored beast for the first forty-two months of the tribulation period and lifts him to great power in the world. This chapter is very harsh and the symbolism hard to explain without offending some people. The location of the harlot is Rome which is called Babylon the great and the mother of harlots and an abomination of the earth. Babylon will be where the false prophet causes the world to worship the anti-Christ as God and causes the world to receive the mark of the beast. The harlot controls the beast for the first forty-two months but in verse sixteen the beast turns on the harlot and destroys her with fire. The beast will move his rule over the earth to Jerusalem to the temple where he lifts himself as God on a throne in the holy of holies. The whole earth will then worship the beast as God and all that do not worship him or his image and receive his mark in their right hand or their forehead will be killed. These are harsh times and these are harsh words in this chapter.

Vs 1-2 **"And there came one of the seven angels which had the seven vials, and**

talked with me, saying unto me, Come hither; I will show unto thee the

judgment of the great whore that sitteth upon many waters: With whom the

kings of the earth have committed fornication, and the inhabitants of the

earth have been made drunk with the wine of her fornication."

One of the seven angels that had the seven bowls of the judgment of God

ties the judgment on religious Babylon and commercial Babylon to the last days

of the tribulation period. This harlot is far worse than the Jezebel in the letter to

the church at Thyatyria in chapter two. Jezebel had committed fornication with

the members of the church, but this harlot has committed fornication with the

entire world. This harlot is comparable to Israel when the Jews worshipped idols

and left their husband Jehovah God by name and were in love with other

husbands or idols. The apostate church has a name that they are Christian but

they worship the anti-Christ or the beast and even worship his image as an idol.

The true bride of Christ has been called out to go to heaven for the marriage feast,

while the harlot is left on the earth. The harlot sits upon many waters which is

explained in verse fifteen. **"And he saith unto me, the waters which thou**

sawest, where the whore sitteth, are peoples, and multitudes, and nations, and

tongues." This tells us that there will be a world church at this time with the

harlot as the leader of the apostate church. All the worlds religions will be

brought under one church with one leader. This is hard to believe that Buddhism,

Mohammedism, atheist, Catholicism, Christianity, Mormonism and all the rest of religion in the world will be brought together under this one world church. The kings of the earth make this religion the state religion with all the world worshipping the anti-Christ as their God. It will be like the whole world is made drunk with intoxication with their desire like fornication with the harlot.

Vs 3 **"So he carried me away in the spirit into the wilderness: and I saw a woman sit upon a scarlet-colored beast, full of names of blasphemy, having seven heads and ten horns."**

This angel carries John into a wilderness on the earth and shows him things that will happen and then explains what he saw. There is a wilderness around Rome which is where the woman is found. Revelation 18:18 **"And the woman which thou sawest is that great city, which reigneth over the kings of the earth."** The woman sits on a scarlet-colored beast with seven heads and ten horns. She is pictured as a rider having control of the beast. Revelation 18:9 **"And here is the mind which hath wisdom. The seven heads are seven mountains, on which the woman sitteth."** The apostate church will be located at Rome. Full of the names of blasphemy refers to every religion in the world will be the name of this one world church.

Vs 4   **"And the woman was arrayed in purple and scarlet color, and decked with gold and precious stones and pearls, having a golden cup in her hand full of abominations and filthiness of her fornication:"**

Scarlet and purple are the colors of this woman with gold and precious stones and pearls on her garments. This is the high and priestly dress of this church leader. This could only be referring to the Roman Catholic church with the all the decoration and buildings lined with gold and precious stones. The false prophet has to come into power through this one world church located at Rome. This woman has a golden cup full of filthiness and fornication. This cup is the sacrament cup and what is in it we do not know. The whole world drinks of this cup with the woman.

Vs 5   **"And upon her forehead was a name written, mystery, Babylon the great, the mother of harlots and abominations of the earth."**

All religions will be found in this apostate church and is called the mother of harlots. She is called mystery Babylon for it truly is a mystery how Satan can cause the world to worship his anti-Christ under all the religions in the world in one world church. This apostate church is an abomination to God in heaven.

Vs 6   "And I saw the woman drunken with the blood of the saints, and with the blood of the martyrs of Jesus: and when I saw her, I wondered with great admiration."

The sacrament cup may be filled with the blood of those killed for their testimony of Jesus Christ and the world drinks from the cup. This is practiced by the Satan worshipers even today. They drink the blood of sacrificed animals or even people in their worship of Satan. This is so horrible to think that this could be the interpretation of this verse.

Vs 7   "And the angel said unto me, wherefore didst thou marvel? I will show thee the mystery of the woman, and of the beast that carrieth her, which hath the seven heads and ten horns."

John's mind does not comprehend what he is seeing. The angel will explain to John what he has seen which reveals the interpretation of much of what John has seen throughout the entire book of Revelation.

Vs 8   "The beast that thou sawest was, and is not; and shall ascend out of the bottomless pit, and go into perdition: and they that dwell on the earth shall wonder, whose names were not written in the book of life from the foundation of the world, when they behold the beast that was, and is not, and yet is."

This is a man that was alive at one time on the earth, was not alive when John wrote the book of Revelation and yet is alive during the tribulation period. The earth will wonder at this man being on the earth and they do not know where he came from. There is no record of his birth and he may be the rider of the white horse that comes at the beginning of the tribulation period. The false prophet may cause the world to believe that he is the Christ returning to this earth to usher in the thousand year reign. This angel reveals to John that this beast ascends out of the bottomless pit and will be cast back into perdition. In chapter thirteen John has revealed that the first beast that rises out of the sea is worshipped by the world and that the second beast that rises out of the earth causes the world to worship him as God and to receive the mark of the first beast. This beast with the seven heads and the ten horns is the anti-Christ and we have already suggested that he may be Judas Iscariot. Satan is an imitator and may have a son just like God had a Son. Acts 1:20 **"For it is written in the book of Psalms, Let his habitation be desolate, and let no man dwell therein: and, his bishopric let another take."** This speaks of Judas having a desolate habitation where no man shall dwell. The bottomless pit is reserved for the fallen angels, the anti-Christ (beast out of the sea) and the false prophet (the beast out of the earth). Judas may be in the bottomless pit waiting to ride back into the earth on a white horse. John 17:12 **"While I was with them in the world, I kept them in thy name: those that thou gavest me I have kept, and none of them is lost, but for the son** of perdition; that the scriptures might be fulfilled." Judas is called the son of

perdition by Jesus Christ and that he is lost. John 6:70 **"Jesus answered them,**

Have I not chosen you twelve, and one of you is a devil?" Judas was part man

and part devil, and the devil part took control of him, to do his fathers will. II

Thessalonians 2:3 **"Let no man deceive you by any means: for that day shall**

not come, except there come a falling away first, and that man of sin be

revealed, the son of perdition." Paul tells us plainly that the man of sin, also

called the anti-Christ and the beast will be the son of Satan. This beast also will

be the eight Roman Caesar to rule over the revived Roman Empire.

Vs 9-11 **"And here is the mind which hath wisdom. The seven heads are seven**

mountains, on which the woman sitteth. And there are seven kings: five are

fallen, and one is, and another is not yet come; and when he cometh, he must

continue a short space. And the beast that was, and is not, even he is the

eight, and is of the seven, and goeth into perdition."

The beast and the woman are located in Rome, which is believed by most

Bible scholars as the city with seven mountains. The city of Rome is also referred

to as the seat of Satan and as Babylon in Revelation. Rome is the location of

religious Babylon in this chapter. The angel explains that there have been five

beast that have fallen, one is at the time John is writing the Revelation and

another beast will rule for a short time. **"And there are seven kings"** is taken by some (including Newell and Govett, who are excellent commentators on Revelation) to mean individual rulers, Govett gives the following list that had fallen before John penned the Revelation:

1.) Julius Caesar- assassinated

2.) Tiberius- poisoned or smothered

3.) Caligula- assassinated

4.) Claudius- poisoned

5.) Nero- committed suicide

"The one is" refers to Domitian who ruled the Roman Empire while John lived and exiled him to the island of Patmos. **"And another is not yet come"** refers to Titus who ruled for just two years before the Roman Empire fell into smaller kingdoms, much like the countries of today. **"And the beast that was, and is not, even he is the eighth"** refers to the final Roman Caesar that shall rule the revived Roman Empire and he shall be cast back into perdition.

Vs 12-13 **"And the ten horns which thou sawest are ten kings, which have received no kingdoms as yet; but receive power as kings one hour with the beast. These have one mind, and shall give their power and strength unto the beast."**

Daniel chapter seven describes this beast that John saw rise up out of the sea and explains how he will gain their support. Out of the ten horns, three will refuse to support the beast and are plucked out by the roots and the rest whole heartedly support him as their one world leader. The seven kings that are left have one mind or the same thought and that is to survive, so they give their power and all their military strength to the beast.

Vs 14 **"These shall make war with the Lamb, and the Lamb shall overcome them: for he is Lord of Lords, and King of Kings: and they that are with him are called, and chosen, and faithful."**

Satan thinks that he has a chance to take the throne away from Jesus when he returns to this earth with the saints of God to rule and reign as King of Kings and Lord of Lords. Satan might think that he got rid of Jesus on the cross of Calvary and with all the power with his army, he will get rid of Jesus again. Satan has a rude awakening coming to him, when his army is totally wiped away when Jesus comes back to this earth.

Vs 15 **"And he saith unto me, The waters which thou sawest, where the whore sitteth, are peoples, and multitudes, and nations, and tongues."**

The beast and the whore rule over all the people that are left on the earth at the end of the tribulation. This verse explains that the beast that rises up out of the sea of all the people on the earth, and the mystery of where he came from is explained by the angel as being from the bottomless pit.

Vs 16 **"And the ten horns which thou sawest upon the beast, these shall hate the whore, and shall make her desolate and naked, and shall eat her flesh, and burn her with fire."**

The letter to the church at Laodicea, which is the apostate church during the tribulation period is warned of this event. Revelation 3:17-18 **"Because thou sayest, I am rich, and increased with goods, and have need of nothing; and knowest not that thou art wretched, and miserable, and poor, and blind, and naked: I counsel thee to buy of me gold tried in the fire, that thou mayest be rich; and white raiment, that thou mayest be clothed, and that the shame of thy nakedness do not appear; and anoint thine eyes with eyesalve, that thou mayest see."** The whore which is that great city of Rome will be burned to the ground and the skeleton will look like the bones of an animal with all the flesh burned away. The beast and the ten kingdoms will hate the whore and no longer need her to have worship by her. She rides the beast at the begining and now the beast turns on her and destroys her with fire. The beast is now worshipped by the world and has been made to receive his mark in their hand or their forehead. The beast has moved his rule to Jerusalem where he sits in the temple to be worshipped as God.

Vs 17 **"For God hath put in their hearts to fulfill his will, and to agree, and give their kingdom unto the beast, until the words of God shall be fulfilled."**

God has a declarative will and a permissive will. The destruction of the whore which is that great city of Rome is God's declarative will and his permissive will. It fulfills God's purpose for the whore to be destroyed. Just like God used Julius Caesar to take a census when Jesus was born, it fulfilled the scriptures that the Savior would be born in Bethlehem. God allows evil nations to do his will and sometimes we do not understand why things in history happen as they do. God used a wicked man like Hitler to bring his people back to Israel to establish them as a nation again. This was a fulfillment of scripture that God would bring back the nation of Israel like the budding of the fig tree and that one generation would not pass away before the end of time would come.

Vs 18 **"And the woman which thou sawest is that great city, which reigneth over the kings of the earth,"**

This great city which shall rule over the earth again is the revived Roman Empire in that great city of Rome.

REVELATION CHAPTER 18

John continues the break from chapter twelve to chapter nineteen where he describes things that have already happened under the seven seals that have already been opened. Chapter seventeen and eighteen reveals the judgment of God on the religious Babylon and the commercial Babylon. Chapter eighteen deals with the judgment of God on commercial Babylon with the great whore that rides on the back of a scarlet colored beast located at Rome. John sees "another angel" come down from heaven and announces the fall of commercial Babylon, then announces the anguish of the world over the fall of their beloved city of Rome and then reveals the joy in heaven because of the judgment on commercial Babylon.

Vs 1   **"And after these things I saw another angel come down from heaven, having great power; and the earth was lightened with his glory."**

John is still on the earth with one of the angels that had the seven bowls of the wrath of God and has seen the judgment on the woman that sat on the scarlet-colored beast. After seeing the judgment on the religious Babylon, John sees "another angel" come from heaven with great power and his glory lightened the earth. This angel could only be Jesus Christ as the light of this world.

Vs 2   **"And he cried mightily with a strong voice, saying, Babylon the great is**

fallen, is fallen, and is become the habitation of devils, and the hold of every

foul spirit, and a cage of every unclean and hateful bird."

The judgment of God on commercial Babylon is carried out by this angel

with great power which John goes back to explain from chapter fourteen.

Revelation 14:6-8 **"And I saw another angel fly in the midst of heaven, having**

the everlasting gospel to preach unto them that dwell on the earth, and to

every nation, and kindred, and tongue, and people. Saying with a loud voice,

Fear God, and give glory to him; for the hour of judgment is come: and

worship him that made heaven, and earth, and the sea, and the fountains of

waters. And there followed another angel, saying, Babylon is fallen, is fallen,

that great city, because she made all nations drink of the wine of the wrath of

her fornication." The destruction of this wicked city is accomplished in one day

and no man will ever dwell there again. Isaiah 13:19-22 **"And Babylon, the**

glory of kingdoms, the beauty of the Chaldees excellency, shall be as when

God overthrew Sodom and Gomorra. It shall never be inhabited, neither

shall it be dwelt in from generation to generation; neither shall the Arabian

pitch his tent there; neither shall the shepherds make their fold there. But

wild beast of the desert shall lie there; and their houses shall be full of doleful

creatures; and owls shall dwell there, and satyrs shall dance there. And the

wild beast of the islands shall cry in their desolate houses, and dragons in

their pleasant palaces; and her time is near to come, and her days shall not be prolonged." Also Jeremiah chapter fifty prophesied of this time of destruction of Babylon. This angel says "Babylon is fallen, is fallen" which is in the past tense. This judgment is just as if it has already happened and is sure to come because God's Word has said it will come to pass.

Vs 3   **"For all nations have drunk of the wine of the wrath of her fornication, and the kings of the earth have committed fornication with her, and the merchants of the earth are waxed rich through the abundance of her delicacies."**

The world is drunk with gluttony and riches that the woman in chapter seventeen has offered them in the cup of her abomination and filthiness. The religious Babylon and commercial Babylon are tied together in the same place. This is when church and state get into the same bed and commit fornication. The corruptness of government will filter into the business and into the religious control of this great city Rome under the power of Satan through the false prophet. This is one reason why the world will worship the anti-Christ, because they love money and power more than they love the Lord Jesus Christ. I John 2:16 **"For all that is in the world, the lust of the flesh, and the lust of the eyes, and the pride of life, is not of the Father, but is of the world."** All sin comes through these three ways to a man. These are the ways Satan allures man away from serving God and during the tribulation period he is working overtime to cause men to love the flesh and not be willing to die for their commitment to Jesus Christ. Men will love things and money that Satan provides to them more than they want the treasures in heaven. Men will love the positions and the power they have under the beast than they desire being a servant of God. This desire for commercial Babylon may be the wine that the kings and all the people are made drunk on. They have sold their soul for the "lust of the flesh, the lust of the eyes and the pride of life."

Vs 4   **"And I heard another voice from heaven, saying, Come out of her, my people, that ye be not partakers of her sins, and that ye receive not her plagues."**

This verse is a mystery in itself. This may refer the resurrection of the saints that were killed for their testimony of Jesus Christ through the seven years of the tribulation. Revelation 20:4 **"And I saw thrones, and they that sat upon them, and judgment was given unto them: and I saw the souls of them that were beheaded for the witness of Jesus, and for the word of God, and which had not worshipped the beast, neither his image, neither had received his mark upon their foreheads, or in their hands; and they lived and reigned with Christ a thousand years."** This verse could pertain to some saints or Jews that are still alive and have not been killed for their testimony of Jesus Christ and are in prison awaiting their execution. All the people on the earth will have to make a decision whether to accept the mark of the beast and bow down and worship the beast or his image or be killed for their testimony of Jesus.

Vs 5-6   **"For her sins have reached unto heaven, and God hath remembered her iniquities. Reward her even as she rewarded you, and double unto her double according to her works: in the cup which she hath filled fill to her double."**

For those who have been tortured and beheaded for the cause of Jesus Christ by the woman or the apostate church at Rome, God will reward the woman double her evil works back unto her. God keeps records of everything that goes on in this world and he remembers every iniquity that the woman and all those evil men that worship the beast and receive his mark. They will suffer in GEHENNA twice as much misery and torture that they inflict on others.

Vs 7   **"How much she hath glorified herself, and lived deliciously, so much torment and sorrow give her; for she saith in her heart, I sit a queen, and am no widow, and shall see no sorrow."**

The religious Babylon located at Rome has glorified herself above the God of heaven and even above the beast that she rides in chapter seventeen. She has lived in luxury needing nothing. Revelation 3:17 **"Because thou sayest, I** am rich, and increased with goods, and have need of nothing; and knowest not that thou art wretched, and miserable, and poor, and blind, and naked." This is the attitude of the apostate church in the letter to the church at Laodicea during the tribulation period. The harlot in chapter seventeen says that she is not a widow and sits as a queen on the seven mountains in Rome. This may be a reference to the anti-Christ as the beast being her husband and he is not dead. This is why God's word calls her a whore. She has a name that she is married to Jesus Christ and claims her husband is the anti-Christ. This harlot says that she is a queen and shall not see sorrow. Her husband, the anti-Christ, is a king and that makes her a queen. When we begin to think that we are on top of the world and lay back and say to ourselves; "lets eat and drink for we have storehouses full and have need of nothing," then watch out, the next thing you will find is the bottom.

Vs 8   **"Therefore shall her plagues come in one day, death, and mourning, and famine; and she shall be utterly burned with fire: for strong is the Lord God who judgeth her."**

It does not take long to come from the top to the bottom. One day is all it takes the beast to burn her with fire to the ground. Revelation 17:16-17 **"And the ten horns which thou sawest upon the beast, these shall hate the whore, and shall make her desolate and naked, and shall eat her flesh, and burn her with fire. For God hath put in their hearts to fulfill his will, and agree, and** give their kingdom unto the beast, until the words of God shall be fulfilled."

The sudden destruction of the woman might be with a nuclear bomb which

causes the whole area to not be inhabited by man again. The ten horns or kings

will hate the whore who rules over them. She has become puffed up with her

power over the earth and the earth now hates the woman. She says that she is a

queen and is not a widow and shall see no sorrow. The beast has by this time

taken control of the world and is worshipped as God, so he no longer needs the

apostate church to tell him what to do and wants to get her off his back.

Revelation 17:3 **"So he carried me away in the spirit into the wilderness: and**

I saw a woman sit upon a scarlet-colored beast." The beast has total power at

this time over the entire world and he does not want to share it with the woman.

Vs 9-10 **"And the kings of the earth, who have committed fornication and lived**

deliciously with her, shall bewail her, and lament for her, when they shall see

the smoke of her burning, Standing afar off for fear of her torment, saying,

Alas, alas, that great city Babylon, that mighty city! For in one hour is thy

judgment come."

This sounds like a contradiction to what has been said in chapter

seventeen. The kings of the earth hate the whore and they are the ones that

destroy her with fire in one hour. Note that the ten kings stand afar off for fear of

her torment. They know she is going to be destroyed and they stand far away from the fallout of her destruction for fear of the radiation. The kings also say that her judgment is come, but they do not lament for her as the religious Babylon, but for the commerce that is lost.

Vs 11-14 **"And the merchants of the earth shall weep and morn over her; for no man buyeth their merchandise any more: The merchandise of gold, and silver, and precious stones, and of pearls, and fine linen, and purple, and silk, and scarlet, and all thyine wood, and all manner vessels of ivory, and all manner vessels of precious wood, and of brass, and iron, and marble, and cinnamon, and odors, and ointments, and frankincense, and wine, and oil, and fine flour, and wheat, and beast, and sheep, and horses, and chariots, and slaves, and souls of men. And the fruits that thy soul lusteth after are departed from thee, and all things which were dainty and goodly are departed from thee, and thou shalt find them no more at all."**

These things are the luxuries in life and not the necessities. The world stock market will be in Rome and all buying and selling of these commodities will be from commercial Babylon in Rome. Even slaves will be sold from commercial Babylon. Those men and women that have run their credit hand over the limit will be sold to pay their debts. Those who have sold their soul in lust for the flesh are sold and bought from commercial Babylon. When the woman is burned with fire, the luxuries will not be found anymore. The automobile dealers will not be able to buy the latest model of chariot anymore. The world monetary system also comes from Rome and the one world currency will come from Rome. The one world currency is going to happen and may occur before the anti-Christ takes power over this world. Many believe that the world currency will be in such a state of fluctuation at the beginning of the tribulation that the anti-Christ will gain his world power from controlling the wealth of the world and instituting a one world currency. There are approximately five men in the world that control the worlds monetary system. They set interest rates in all the countries and actually hold the notes on the indebtedness of all the nations. The anti-Christ may rise to power through one of these five men. The nations of this world would find it hard to disagree with his terms when they owe him all those billions of dollars.

Vs 15-19 **"The merchants of these things, which were made rich by her, shall stand afar off for fear of her torment, weeping and wailing, and saying , Alas, alas, that great city, that was clothed in fine linen, and purple, and scarlet, and decked with gold, and precious stones, and pearls! For in one hour so great riches is come to naught. And every shipmaster, and all the company in ships, and sailors, and as many as trade by sea, stood afar off, and cried when they saw the smoke of her burning, saying, What city is like unto this great city! And they cast dust on their heads, and cried, weeping and wailing,** saying, Alas, alas, that great city, wherein were made rich all that had ships in the sea by reason of her costliness! For in one hour is she made desolate."

We see two groups of people on the earth that mourn the destruction of commercial Babylon. The merchants who were made rich by buying and selling through the great city of Rome. They had a total financial loss when their goods went up in smoke. They are not morning the religious Babylon, but the commercial Babylon. The ship masters, the sailors, the ship owners and all the passengers moan because of the pleasures they are going to miss in commercial Babylon. They do not miss religious Babylon either. What city can they go to now that is like that great city of Rome. Again their only concern was that they no longer had that great city of Rome to satisfy their "lust of the flesh, the lust of the eyes and the pride of life." They no longer have a purpose for living, their God had destroyed that great city of Rome.

Vs 20-21 **"Rejoice over her, thou heaven, and ye holy apostles and prophets; for God hath avenged you on her. And a mighty angel took up a stone like a great millstone, and cast it into the sea, saying, Thus with violence shall that great city Babylon be thrown down, and shall be found no more at all."**

This verse is the fulfillment of the prophesy of Daniel about the dream of king Nebuchadnezzar. Daniel 2:31-35 **"Thou, O king, sawest, and behold a** great image. This great image, whose brightness was excellent, stood before thee; and the form thereof was terrible. This image's head was of fine gold, his breast and his arms of silver, his belly and his thighs of brass, his legs of iron, his feet part of iron and part of clay. Thou sawest till a stone was cut out without hands, which smote the image upon his feet that were of iron and clay, and brake them to pieces. Then was the iron, the clay, the brass, the silver, and the gold, broken to pieces together, and became like the chaff of the summer threshing floors; and the wind carried them away, that no place was found for them: and the stone that smote the image became a great mountain, and filled the whole earth." King Nebuchadnezzar was shown the world powers that would be till the end of time on this earth. The world power of the iron feet and iron mixed with clay toes represented the revival of the Roman Empire which was the iron legs. The ten toes represents the ten kings that give their power to the anti-Christ. The stone that was cut out without hands is the last world power that shall rule for eternity. The mill stone falls on the feet of the beast and breaks them to pieces. The stone then falls on the whole beast and is ground to powder and is blown away to never be seen again. This verse in Revelation is the fulfillment of the stone that crushes the world kingdom of the anti-Christ. Like a great stone cast into the water, makes a big splash and the ripples go away from where it is cast till the ripples disappear. The stone is no longer seen and the evidence of the stone being there vanishes like the ripples. The stone will not be seen again. This is the picture of this great city of Rome.

Vs 22-23 **"And the voice of harpers, and musicians, and of pipers, and trumpeters, shall be heard no more at all in thee; and no craftsman, of whatsoever craft he be, shall be found in thee; and the sound of a millstone shall be heard no more at all in thee; and the light of a candle shall shine no more at all in thee; and the voice of the bridegroom and of the bride shall be heard no more at all in thee: For thy merchants were great men of the earth; for by thy sorceries were all nations deceived."**

As in the explanation of the second verse of this chapter the great city of Rome and the surrounding wilderness will become a prison or a cage for all the dirty animals of this world and will never be inhabited by man again. This area will be contaminated for the thousand year reign of Christ on this earth. This leads us to believe that the anti-Christ used a nuclear bomb to destroy the woman or that great city of Rome which is called Babylon. This may be the explanation of the destruction of that great city in one hour.

Vs 24 **"And in her was found the blood of prophets, and of saints, and of all that were slain upon the earth."**

This wicked city from it's founding before Christ was born to the destruction during the tribulation period has shed the blood of prophets, of saints and all those slain during the tribulation period. We know that Paul was killed in Rome for his testimony of Jesus. There were countless Christians killed for sport by lions in the arenas during the first Roman Empire in this great city of Rome. During the tribulation period this great city of Rome may be the execution place for all who refuse to worship the beast or his image or receive his mark in their forehead or their hands.

REVELATION CHAPTER 19

The scene has changed back to heaven from the earth where John was taken by one of the angels with the seven bowls of the judgment of God in chapters seventeen and eighteen. God has judged the whore that rides on a scarlet-colored beast with seven heads and ten horns and put his will into the beast to destroy the woman. We saw that the woman was that great city called Babylon and will be the city of Rome as the seat of the anti-Christ where he rules the world. We also saw that the anti-Christ as the beast with seven heads and ten horns moved his kingdom to Jerusalem to the temple of God where he sits in the holy of holies in the temple proclaiming himself as God. The anti-Christ no longer needs religious Babylon in Rome because he has complete control over the world and all people are forced to wear his mark and fall down and worship him or his image as God. The anti-Christ rules the world from the temple in Jerusalem from the middle of the tribulation to the end of the last forty-two months when he destroys the woman in one hour and burns her with fire. In chapter nineteen, John picks up from chapter eleven with the coming of Jesus Christ as King of kings and Lord of lords returning to this earth to set up his thousand year reign on the earth.

Vs 1   **"And after these things, I heard a great voice of much people in heaven, saying, Alleluia; Salvation, and glory, and honor, and power, unto the Lord our God:"**

This is the first time in the Bible that the word "Alleluia" is used which means praise the Lord. "Alleluia" is used four times in this chapter. After all these things from the opening of the first seal of the seven sealed scroll to the judgments of God on religious Babylon and commercial Babylon, John is back in heaven viewing the preparation of the return of Jesus Christ to the earth as King of kings and Lord of lords. There is a great multitude in heaven that praise Jesus.

Vs 2-3 **"For true and righteous are his judgments: for he hath judged the great whore, which did corrupt the earth with her fornication, and hath avenged the blood of his servants at her hand. And again they said, Alleluia, and her smoke rose up for ever and ever."**

Revelation 14:8-11 "And there followed another angel, saying , Babylon is fallen, is fallen, that great city, because she made all nations drink of the wine of the wrath of her fornication. And the third angel followed them, saying with a loud voice, If any man worship the beast and his image and receive his mark in his forehead, or his hand, the same shall drink of the wine of the wrath of God, which is poured out without mixture into the cup of his indignation; and he shall be tormented with fire and brimstone in the presence of the holy angels, and in the presence of the Lamb: And the smoke of their torment ascendeth up for ever and ever: and they have no rest day nor night, who worship the beast and his image, and whosoever receiveth the

mark of the beast." Before the coming of Jesus Christ as Lord of lords and King

of kings, there will have been millions of people already killed through the

plagues and judgments of God upon those who worship the beast and wear his

mark. The picture of her smoke rising for ever and ever is that of hell with all

those that have already been killed with those that were in that great city of

Babylon when she was destroyed. The rest of those who wear the mark of the

beast will be killed in that great battle of Armageddon and they also will be cast

into Hell.

Vs 4-5 **"And the four and twenty elders and the four beast fell down and**

worshipped God that sat on the throne, saying, Amen: Alleluia. And a voice

came out of the throne, saying, Praise our God, all ye servants, and ye that

fear him, both small and great."

This may be the alleluia chorus that we know that is sung in heaven. It is

the most beautiful song that I know. Praise breaks out in heaven. If it were not

for the blood of Jesus that was shed for our sins and our faith in Jesus as the Son

of God, we would be in Hell. This praise is directed to Jesus Christ for what he

did for us on the cross of Calvary.

Vs 6-7 **"And I heard as it were the voice of a great multitude, and as the voice of**

many waters, and as the voice of mighty thunderings, saying, Alleluia: for the

Lord God omnipotent reigneth. Let us be glad and rejoice, and give honor to him: for the marriage of the Lamb is come, and his wife hath made herself ready."

Jesus will come for his bride in the rapture, when he takes the bride to meet his Father in heaven. The marriage feast may last for the seven years of the tribulation period and then Jesus will take his bride back to the earth to live with him for a thousand years. This event in heaven is preparation for the bridegroom to take his bride and they go to live together for ever and ever. The wife has made herself ready to go on the honeymoon with her husband for a thousand years. In chapter twenty-one and twenty-two John describes the new heaven and the new earth where the bride will live with her Husband for ever and ever.

Vs 8-9 **"And to her was granted that she should be arrayed in fine linen, clean and white: for fine linen is the righteousness of the saints. And he saith unto me, Write, Blessed are they which are called unto the marriage supper of the Lamb. And he saith unto me, These are the true sayings of God."**

The marriage supper is the last event in heaven before the Bridegroom leaves with his bride. Blessed are they who are the called unto the marriage supper. The true church is the bride that has been called from the time that Jesus rose from the grave till the time he comes for his bride. John sees a great multitude singing alleluia to Jesus. Matthew 25:1-13 **"Then shall the kingdom of heaven be likened unto ten virgins, which took their lamps, and went forth to meet the bridegroom. And five of them were wise, and five were foolish. They that were foolish took their lamps, and took no oil with them: But the wise took oil in their vessels with their lamps. While the bridegroom tarried, they all slumbered and slept. And at midnight there was a cry made, Behold, the bridegroom cometh; go ye out to meet him. Then all those virgins arose, and trimmed their lamps. And the foolish said unto the wise, Give us of your oil; for our lamps are gone out. But the wise answered, saying, Not so; lest there be not enough for us and you: but go ye rather to them that sell, and buy for yourselves. And while they went to buy, the bridegroom came; and they that were ready went in with him to the marriage: and the door was shut. Afterward came also the other virgins, saying, Lord, Lord, open to us. But he answered and said, Verily I say unto you, I know you not. Watch therefore, for ye know neither the day nor the hour wherein the Son of man cometh."** Jesus gives us a picture of the rapture of the bride when he comes in the air for the true church. The true church is like the virgins that have oil in their vessels. The apostate church is like the virgins that took no oil at all. They were all expecting the bridegroom to come, but as time went by they all slept. When the bridegroom who is Jesus Christ comes in the air, those that are ready with oil in their lamps will be taken into the marriage with the bridegroom and the door will be shut. The oil represents the Holy Spirit which indwells all those who confess Jesus as their Lord and Savior. This parable teaches us that there are

many that are in the church that trust in something other than the Lord Jesus

Christ and what he did for us on the cross of Calvary. They may think that being

a member of this church or that church saves them, or that they were baptized

when a baby saves them, or their giving money saves them, or their praying to one

of the saints or the mother of Jesus saves them. Acts 4:12 **"Neither is there**

salvation in any other: for there is none other name under heaven given

among men, whereby we must be saved." The true bride is the ones that trust in

Jesus Christ and look for his coming in the air to take them to the marriage in

heaven.

Vs 10 **"And I fell at his feet to worship him. And he said unto me, See thou do it**

not: I am thy fellow servant, and of thy brethren that have the testimony of

Jesus: worship God: for the testimony of Jesus is the spirit of prophecy."

We are not told who is talking to John in heaven, but this man tells John

that he is a fellow servant of Jesus Christ and a Jew. This may be John in the

resurrected body talking to John in the flesh telling him what to write in the

Revelation. John is still in the flesh in heaven, being shown the things that must

shortly come to pass. His flesh is weak and he does not have perfect

understanding of all that he sees. When we all get to heaven, we will know even

as we are known. We will understand everything and know everyone without being told. John does not even know to whom he is talking. There is only one who deserves our worship in this entire universe.

THE RIDER ON A WHITE HORSE

John picks back up from where he left off in the sequence of events from chapter eleven with the temple of God being opened in heaven with lightning's, and voices, and thundering, and an earthquake, and great hail.

Vs 11 **"And I saw heaven opened, and behold a white horse; and he that sat upon him was called Faithful and True, and in righteousness he doth judge and make war."**

The scene opens in heaven with Jesus Christ riding on a white horse returning to the earth to make war with the forces of Satan, the anti-Christ and the false prophet on the earth. The battle of Armageddon will be a short one with Christ against the whole world's armies. Jesus rides a white horse which is the animal of war. When Jesus entered Jerusalem, he rode on an ass, which is the animal of kings. Jesus is returning to earth this time to put down all unrighteousness and to be judge, jury and executioner of those who are unrighteous.

JESUS CHRIST HAS FOUR NAMES

1.) "Called Faithful and True": Like the gospel writer Mark, who saw Jesus as the servant of God. Jesus was faithful and true to do the will of God the Father to leave heaven in all its splendor and leave his place as the Son of God ruling over the entire universe to come to earth as a mere man to become a servant. Mark portrayed Jesus coming to the earth as a servant of God to die for the entire lost world.

2.) "He had a name written, that no man knew": Like the gospel writer Luke, who saw Jesus as a man. Jesus was the Son of God, but yet a man with living flesh and blood tempted just like we are tempted by the flesh. Jesus was a perfect man without sin living a perfect life. This name that no man knew was the name of his Father in heaven and not the name given to him on this earth.

3.) "Called the Word of God": Like the gospel writer John, who saw Jesus as the Christ, the Savior, the Son of God and the Messiah. Jesus satisfied the prophesy of the scriptures in fulfilling the Word of God. He was the promised seed to Eve in the garden and the promised seed to faithful Abraham that would take away the sins of the world.

4.) "He had a name written, King of Kings, and Lord of Lords: Like the gospel writer Matthew, who saw Jesus as the deliverer that would rule over the nations for ever and ever. This is the picture of Jesus coming back to this earth to rule over his people for eternity.

Vs 12 **"His eyes were as a flame of fire, and on his head were many crowns; and he had a name written, that no man knew, but he himself."**

His eyes have a fire in them that will judge the nations on this earth. He wears many crowns which represents many kingdoms are all going to be ruled by Jesus. The nations on this earth have rejected him and now he will judge them. The sentence has been pronounced by God the Father on all them that worship the beast and his image and have received the mark of the beast in their forehead or their hand.

Vs 13 **"And he was clothed with a vesture dipped in blood: and his name is called The Word of God."**

Isaiah 63:2-4 **"Wherefore art thou red in thine apparel, and thy garments like him that treadeth in the winefat? I have trodden the winepress alone; and of the people there are none with me: for I will tread them in mine anger, and trample them in my fury; and their blood shall be sprinkled upon my garments, and I will stain all my raiment. For the day of vengeance is in mine heart, and the year of my redeemed is come."** Jesus wars with armies of the world by himself and is pictured as a harvest of the vineyard with a sickle in his hand.

Vs 14 **"And the armies which were in heaven followed him upon white horses, clothed in fine linen, white and clean."**

The bride that has been taken to heaven for the marriage now is pictured with her husband returning to the earth on white horses. The bride is called an army following Jesus which may represent the union of a husband and a wife as becoming one flesh. Ephesians 5:29-32 **"For no man ever yet hated his own flesh; but nouresheth and cherisheth it, even as the Lord the church: For we are members of his body, of his flesh, and of his bones. For this cause shall a man leave his father and mother, and shall be joined unto his wife, and they two shall be one flesh. This is a great mystery: but I speak concerning Christ and the church."** The bride is with her husband and both are at war with the forces of Satan on this earth. There will be horses in heaven and maybe a lot of other animals. Christ rides on a white horse and the bride rides on white horses. Notice that the bride has on fine linen, white and clean. The bide does not fight in the battle of Armageddon.

Vs 15 "And out of his mouth goeth a sharp sword, that with it he should smite the
nations: and he shall rule them with a rod of iron: and he treadeth the
winepress of the fierceness and wrath of Almighty God."

Hebrews 4:12 "For the word of God is quick, and powerful, and
sharper than any two-edged sword, piercing even to the dividing asunder of
soul and spirit, and of the joints and marrow, and is a discerner of the
thoughts and intents of the heart." The sword of Jesus mouth is like a two-
edged sword that can cut both ways. It can cut to the very thoughts of the saints
of God in their motives and real service to Jesus Christ revealing the love in our
hearts to God and to our fellow man. It also can cut the sinner to pieces revealing
to him that he needs a Savior to pay for his sins, for his very best he can do is like
repugnant filthy rags in his sight. The Word of God is all powerful and we can
use the word of God to have victory over Satan in our daily lives. The words of
Jesus when he battles the armies of Satan in the battle of Armageddon will cut
them to pieces. Jesus will speak and what he says will come to pass immediately.
Jesus will squash the armies of Satan like a ripe grape in the winepress of the
wrath of God.

Vs 16 "And he hath on his vesture and on his thigh a name written, King of Kings,
and Lord of Lords."

Jesus is returning to this earth, not as the savior when he first came, but as King of Kings and as Lord of Lords which will be his name for eternity.

Vs 17-18 "And I saw an angel standing in the sun; and he cried with a loud voice, saying to all the fowls that fly in the midst of heaven, come and gather yourselves together unto the supper of the great God; That ye may eat the flesh of kings, and the flesh of captains, and the flesh of mighty men, and the flesh of horses, and of them that sit upon them, and the flesh of all men, both free and bond, both small and great."

There will be dead men all over the earth, not just at the battle of Armageddon, but all men on the earth are killed. No one knows the lies that the anti-Christ has told to the men on the earth to cause them to war with Jesus Christ. They obviously believe that the anti-Christ is all powerful and can conquer Jesus Christ. The nations of the world have already said "Who is like unto the beast? Who is able to make war with him?" I John 4:1-3 **"Beloved, believe not every spirit, but try the spirits whether they are of God: because many false prophets are gone out into the world. Hereby know ye the Spirit of God: Every spirit that confesseth that Jesus Christ is come in the flesh is of God: And every spirit that confesseth not that Jesus Christ is come in the flesh is not of God: and this is that spirit of anti-Christ, whereof ye have heard that it should come; and even now already is it in the world."** The judgment of God will fall upon all who do not confess that Jesus is the Son of God that came in the flesh and died on the cross of Calvary for their sins and that he rose from the dead on the third day.

Vs 19-21 **"And I saw the beast, and the kings of the earth, and their armies, gathered together to make war against him that sat on the horse, and against his army. And the beast was taken, and with him the false prophet that wrought miracles before him, with which he deceived them that had received the mark of the beast, and them that worshipped his image. These both were cast alive into a lake of fire burning with brimstone. And the remnant were slain with the sword of him that sat upon the horse, which sword proceeded out of his mouth: and all the fowls were filled with their flesh."**

HADES:

We have three places that are referred to as hell in the Bible. There is Hades where all men that die without Jesus Christ are cast. Luke 16:22-31 **"And it came to pass, that the beggar died, and was carried by the angels into Abraham's bosom: the rich man also died, and was buried; and in hell he lift up his eyes, being in torments, and seeth Abraham afar off, and Lazarus in his bosom. And he cried and said, Father Abraham, have mercy on me, and send Lazarus, that he may dip the tip of his finger in water, and cool my tongue; for I am tormented in this flame. But Abraham said, Son, remember** that thou in thy lifetime receivest thy good things, and likewise Lazarus evil

things: but now he is comforted, and thou art tormented. **And besides all this,**

between us and you there is a great gulf fixed: so that they which would pass

from hence to you cannot; neither can they pass to us, that would come from t

hence. Then he said, I pray thee therefore, father, that thou wouldest send

him to my father's house: For I have five brethren; that he may testify unto

them, lest they also come into this place of torment. Abraham saith unto him,

They have Moses and the prophets; let them hear them. And he said, Nay,

Father Abraham: but if one went unto them from the dead, they will repent.

And he said unto him, If they hear not Moses and the prophets, neither will

they be persuaded, though one rose from the dead." Jesus gives us a picture of

Hades where all the dead went before Jesus died on the cross and paid the sin

debt with his own blood. We see a comfortable side and a torment side of Hades.

Those who were saved before Jesus actually died on the cross of Calvary were

saved on credit. Their faith in the promise of God that a Savior would come was

accredited to their account and their spirit and soul was held in the comfortable

side of Hades with father Abraham. Those who died without faith in the

promised seed that would come and take the sins of the world away through his

shed blood were cast into the torment side of Hades. We are also told that there is

a great gulf fixed between the two places and no one could go between the two.

When Jesus died, he descended into Hades where he preached unto those in the

torment side of Hades. I Peter 3:19 **"By which also he went and preached unto** the spirits in prison." When Jesus rose from the grave, he delivered those from the comfortable side of Hades and took them with him to heaven where all the dead in Christ go now since he has paid their sin debt on the cross of Calvary. Ephesians 4:8-10 **"Wherefore he saith, When he ascended up on high, he led captivity captive, and gave gifts unto men. Now that he ascended, what is it but that he also descended first into the lower parts of the earth? He that descended is the same also that ascended up far above all heavens, that he might fill all things."** Now when a saved person dies, his soul and spirit go to be with Jesus in heaven, waiting for that glorious day of resurrection when they will receive a new body like Jesus and their soul and spirit will be placed into that new body. The unbelieving lost man still dies and is cast into the torment side of Hades waiting for that great day when the grave shall give up the dead and they stand in front of the Great White Throne of Jesus Christ to be judged for their wickedness and then cast in GEHENNA for eternal punishment in the fire and brimstone judgment.

GEHENNA:

This verse in Revelation tells us that the first two occupants of GEHENNA are the anti-Christ or the beast that rose up out of the sea and the false prophet or the beast that rises up out of the earth. **"These both were cast alive into a lake of fire burning with brimstone"** and are the first to be cast into GEHENNA. In chapter twenty we will see the rest of the dead brought up out of

Hades and the grave gives up their bodies and they stand before the Great White Throne judgment and are judged for their sins and then cast into GEHENNA for eternity. This happens at the end of the thousand year reign of Jesus on this earth.

THE BOTTOMLESS PIT:

The bottomless pit is the place of torment for the fallen angels that rebelled against God with Satan. Jude 6 **"And the angels which kept not their first estate, but left their own habitation, he hath reserved in everlasting chains under darkness unto the judgment of the great day."** These are the angels that cohabited with the daughters of men and giants were born on the earth before the flood. Man became so corrupted that he destroyed the earth with a flood. There is another we have already discussed that is reserved in the bottomless pit till that day he is let out in the tribulation period. The anti-Christ will come out of the bottomless pit.

REVELATION CHAPTER 20

There are three schools of thought concerning the Millennium or thousand year reign of Jesus Christ:

1.) <u>Post-millennial</u>: This group believed that man would get better and better till Jesus Christ would come at the end of a thousand years of peace on the earth. This theory went out the window with WW I and WW II. Man is actually getting worse and worse. Jesus told us in scripture that as it were in the days of Sodom and Gomorra, so shall it be in the time of his return to this earth. Again he said as it were in the days of Noah, so shall it be in the time of his return to this earth. This world will again have sexual desires running rampant with the homosexual and heterosexual leaving the natural use of the woman and the man leaving the principals set down in marriage by the Bible. We can see this every day in the world today leading us to believe that time is at hand for the return of Jesus Christ.

2.) <u>Ah-millennial</u>: This group spiritualize the book of Revelation to fit into all of history like a crazy puzzle. They believe that man is living in the millennium and Christ is here spiritually ruling this world. They fail to explain how sin is running rampant in this world. Satan has not been bound and cast into the bottomless pit as far as I can see. Even if Revelation is spiritualized and man is living in the thousand years reign, they fail to explain when the thousand years

began and when it ends and where is Jesus Christ.

3.) Pre-millennial: This group takes Revelation just as it reads with Jesus Christ

coming in the air to rapture the saints of God out of this earth with the earth going

through seven years of tribulation and then the return of Jesus Christ to this earth

for a thousand year reign as King of Kings and Lord of Lords.

The Millennium can not begin until:

a.) Satan is bound and cast into the bottomless pit. Revelation 20:2-3

b.) The rapture has to occur. Revelation 4:1

c.) The rapture of the tribulation saints. Revelation 20:4

d.) The curse of sin is removed. Isaiah 11:6-9; 35:1-10; Romans 8:18-23

SATAN IS BOUND FOR A THOUSAND YEARS

Vs 1-3 **"And I saw an angel come down from heaven, having the key of the**

bottomless pit and a great chain in his hand. And he laid hold on the dragon,

that old serpent, which is the Devil, and Satan, and bound him a thousand

years, and cast him into the bottomless pit, and shut him up, and set a seal

upon him, that he should deceive the nations no more, till the thousand years

should be fulfilled: and after that he must be loosed a little season."

The anti-Christ and the false prophet are cast in GEHENNA at the end of chapter nineteen. Now Satan is bound with a chain and cast into the bottomless pit. The bottomless pit is a holding cage for the fallen angels and the beast that is called the anti-Christ at this time now, but during the thousand year reign of Jesus Christ as King of Kings and Lord of Lords, Satan will be the occupant of the bottomless pit. Revelation 1:18 **"I am he that liveth, and was dead; and behold, I am alive for evermore, Amen; and have the keys of hell and of death."** We may identify who cast Satan into the bottomless pit by who has the keys. There is a belief that the keys of heaven and hell were given to Peter and they were handed down from Peter to a Pope to Pope. Notice Jesus has the keys. He binds Satan and cast him into the bottomless pit. Jesus unlocked the door for access to heaven when he rose from the grave and delivered those who were in the comfortable side of Hades and took father Abraham and all the saints there to heaven. Those who have trusted in Jesus Christ today and have died have access to heaven immediately when they die through their faith in him. Romans 10:9-13 **"That if thou shalt confess with thy mouth the Lord Jesus, and shalt believe in thine heart that God hath raised him from the dead, thou shalt be saved. For with the heart man believeth unto righteousness; and with the mouth confession is made unto salvation. For the scripture saith, Whosoever believeth on him shall not be ashamed. For there is no difference between the Jew and the Greek: for the same Lord over all is rich unto all that call upon**

him. For whosoever shall call upon the name of the Lord shall be saved."
The key opening heaven to all men is their faith in Jesus Christ. The key that
opens hell is in the hand of Jesus Christ right now, and forever.

The question of why Satan is allowed to roam the earth today and why he
is loosed at the end of the thousand year reign of Jesus may be asked by man.
Romans 9:20 **"Nay but, O man, who art thou that repliest against God? Shall**
the thing formed say to him that formed it, Why hast thou made me thus?"
God's thinking and God's long-suffering is beyond finding out by man. It may be
that God allows Satan to roam this earth tempting man to not follow God and to
live in sin and reject God's will in his life. Man is a sinner and it is in his nature
to continue sinning, but God wants man to trust in his Son Jesus Christ and to
change his will to not sin. Man makes the choice to follow God's will or to
follow Satan's will to sin. In order to determine the destination of man to an
eternal heaven or to an eternal hell, man has to make a choice. God gave man the
free will to make this choice. Satan is allowed to roam this earth to see which
will man will choose. The same thing will be true at the end of the thousand year
reign of Jesus Christ. Man will have lived on this earth for a thousand years
under perfect conditions with no Satan, with no curse on the ground, with no
death, and with Jesus ruling and reigning over this earth in perfect peace. At the
end of the thousand years there will be a population explosion on this earth with
the 144,000 Jews and all their children living without death and sickness. The

144,000 have already trusted in Jesus Christ as their Lord and Savior during the tribulation period. Their children have seen Jesus as God's Son reigning on this earth for a thousand years and they must make a decision to trust in him or not to trust in him. Satan is let out of the bottomless pit to roam this earth once again to tempt man to follow Satan or to follow Jesus. The sad truth is that there will be a vast number of these children that will follow Satan after the lust of the flesh, the lust of the eye and the pride of life temptations. This is the way all sin is offered to man by Satan. After all mankind has made a choice of whom he will follow, then the end of this earth and all flesh will be destroyed. The philosophy of man is a product of his environment is totally blown out the window with Revelation chapter twenty. This proves that man has a sinful nature and it up to man to change his will and follow Jesus Christ or continue living in sin. Man has to make a choice. Jeremiah 17:9 **"The heart is deceitful above all things, and desperately wicked: who can know it?"** This word "desperately" means incurable. I have seen children come from very poor backgrounds and broken homes that have turned out to be some of the finest adults in our society today. I also have seen children come from ideal homes that have rebelled against everything good that our society stands for. Each person makes a decision to follow after God or to follow after his sinful nature. All mankind needs redemption and that comes only from Jesus Christ.

Vs 4   **"And I saw thrones, and they sat upon them, and judgment was given unto them: and I saw the souls of them that were beheaded for the witness of Jesus, and for the Word of God, and which had not worshipped the beast, neither his image, neither had received his mark upon their foreheads, or in their hands; and they lived and reigned with Christ a thousand years."**

There is another resurrection of those who have trusted in Jesus Christ that have died during the seven years of tribulation. Those who are in this resurrection are listed in this verse. They have given their lives for their testimony of Jesus, the Word of God and have rejected the beast and refused to worship him. They have been beheaded may mean that the guillotine is used to kill all those that refuse to worship the beast during the tribulation period. All the saints in heaven are going to rule and reign with Jesus Christ on this earth for a thousand years. Who are the saints and Jesus going to reign over? The 144,000 Jews that have the seal of God in their foreheads will be protected through the tribulation period and be left on this earth at the end of the seven years. The 144,000 may be children that are taken into the thousand year reign because they were called virgins during the tribulation period. They are now three and one half years older than when they were sealed with the seal of God.

Vs 5-6   **"But the rest of the dead lived not again until the thousand years were finished. This is the first resurrection. Blessed and holy is he that hath part**

**in the first resurrection: on such the second death hath no power, but they
shall be priest of God and of Christ, and shall reign with him a thousand
years."**

All the saints of God that were in the first resurrection when Jesus comes
in the air at the beginning of the tribulation and these who are resurrected from
the dead at the end of the tribulation period will not go through the second death.
John tells us that these are blessed and holy who have been part of the first
resurrection and will reign with Jesus for a thousand years. The rest of the dead
will be in the second resurrection at the end of the thousand years. This will be
the resurrection of the lost who will stand before the white throne judgment and
be cast into GEHENNA with the anti-Christ, the false prophet and Satan.

Vs 7-8 **"And when the thousand years are expired, Satan shall be loosed out of his
prison, and shall go out to deceive the nations which are in the four quarters
of the earth, Gog and Magog, to gather them together to battle: the number
of whom is as the sand of the sea."**

The children of the 144,000 are living under ideal conditions and know
that Jesus sits on a throne ruling over the entire earth as the Son of God. The
saints that come back with Jesus from heaven will have ruled with Jesus over this
earth for a thousand years. These children will have seen the saints worship Jesus

as the Son of God that shed his blood for the sins of the world. The children have

the free will to worship Jesus or to live their lives as they wish serving the flesh

and the desires of the flesh. Parents like today can not make their children

believe in Jesus as the Son of God, they have to decide for themselves. Satan is

let out of his prison for a short time to roam the earth again to deceive the nations

to cause the children to decide whether to follow Jesus or to follow Satan. It is

hard to believe that so many of the children of the 144,000 Jews rebel against all

they have been told and what they have seen for a thousand years and follow the

lies of Satan and make war against Jesus Christ.

Vs 9 **"And they went up on the breadth of the earth, and compassed the camp of**

the saints about, and the beloved city: and fire came down from God out of

heaven, and devoured them."

This army that Satan leads against Jesus Christ and all the saints does not

want to be ruled over but wants to rule themselves. The army come from an area

in the north of Jerusalem called Gog and Magog. They compassed the city of

Jerusalem ready to attack when God from heaven devours them with fire and

brimstone. This gathering of all the saints in Jerusalem may be on a worship day

and Satan tries again to take the throne of Jesus. This has been Satan's plan from

the beginning when he rebelled against God, he desires to be worshipped as God.

This is the last time that Satan is allowed to try and dethrone Jesus and magnify himself as God. All those that follow Satan are killed and devoured by a fire from heaven.

Vs 10 **"And the Devil that deceived them was cast into the lake of fire and brimstone, where the beast and the false prophet are, and shall be tormented day and night for ever and ever."**

The first three occupants of GEHENNA are Satan, the anti-Christ and the false prophet. The world view of Satan today is in Hell where he torments the men that are cast there. Satan is like a roaring lion roaming this earth seeking to devour mankind and cause men to rebel against God and against Jesus Christ and to destroy the Jew. The picture of Satan was painted for us in Revelation chapter twelve. Satan hates the woman which is the nation of Israel and he hates the child of the woman which is Jesus Christ. Satan will be cast into GEHENNA at the end of the thousand year reign of Jesus Christ. There is no escape from GEHENNA and all that are cast into it will be tormented day and night for ever and ever.

THE GREAT WHITE THRONE JUDGMENT

Vs 11 **"And I saw a great white throne, and him that sat on it, from whose face the earth and the heaven fled away: and there was found no place for them."**

This is the time Jesus separates the sheep from the goats and all the dead will brought back to life in the second resurrection. Matthew 25:31-34, 46 **"When the Son of man shall come in his glory, and all the holy angels with him, then shall he sit upon the throne of his glory: And before him shall be gathered all nations: and he shall separate them one from another, as a shepherd divideth his sheep from the goats: And he shall set the sheep on his right hand, but the goats on the left. Then shall the King say into them on his right hand, Come, ye blessed of my Father, inherit the kingdom prepared for you from the foundation of the world: - - - And these shall go away into everlasting punishment: but the righteous into life eternal."** John 5:25-29 **"Verily, verily, I say unto you, The hour is coming, and now is, when the dead shall hear the voice of the Son of God: and they that hear shall live. For as the Father hath life in himself; so hath he given to the Son to have life in himself; And hath given him authority to execute judgment also, because he is the Son of man. Marvel not at this: for the hour is coming, in which all that are in the graves shall hear his voice, and shall come forth; they that have done good, unto the resurrection of life; and they that have done evil, unto the resurrection of damnation."** Jesus is the one who sits on the great white throne to judge the world. John 3:17-19 **"For God sent not his Son into the world to condemn the world; but that the world through him might be saved. He that believeth on him is not condemned: but he that believeth not is condemned already, because he hath not believed in the name of the only**

begotten Son of God." Jesus does not condemn man but passes judgment already decreed by God that all who do not believe in the only begotten Son of God is condemned already. Man makes the choice while alive on the earth to either accept this truth or reject the truth that Jesus is the only begotten Son of God and that he died on the cross of Calvary and that he rose again from the dead on the third day.

Vs 12-13 **"And I saw the dead, small and great, stand before God; and the books were opened, and another book was opened, which is the book of life: and the dead were judged out of those things which were written in the books, according to their works. And the sea gave up the dead which were in it; and death and hell delivered up the dead which were in them: and they were judged every man according to their works."**

The status of a man in this life makes no difference to God. Kings and the poorest of the poor will stand before the great white throne judgment to give account of how they lived their life. The book of life will be opened and their name will not be there. This the Lambs book of life and all that profess Jesus as their Lord and Savior will have their names in this book. The lost are in the second resurrection and their names are not in the Lambs book of life and they will be shown that it is not there. The books of works will be opened and each man and woman will stand there and have their works of the flesh played back to them. A man might say "I did not do that!" The books do not lie and even the intent of the heart is recorded there. God is not prejudiced and is just and only the truth will be revealed to those that stand there. A mans position and wealth will mean nothing and he will not escape the truth. Acts 2:15 **"That there shall be a resurrection of the dead, both of the just and the unjust."**

The sea is referred to as the grave where the body has been placed and the soul and the spirit have gone to Hades to be punished in torment in the flames. Death and Hades delivers up those that are in them. This is referred to as the second resurrection of the dead where the grave and Hades gives up their dead and they receive a new body that shall never die. This new body will have the same desires of hunger and thirst of the fleshly body and their soul and spirit will be placed into their new bodies. Paul gave us the explanation of the resurrection of the dead in I Corinthians chapter fifteen. All those in Hades are delivered up to stand at the great white throne judgment to give account of their works.

Vs 14-15 **"And death and hell were cast into the lake of fire. This is the second death. And whosoever was not found written in the book of life was cast into the lake of fire."**

Death is the body and hell is the soul and spirit that are cast into GEHENNA which is called the second death. You have heard the phrase that if you are born twice then you only die once and if you are born once then you die twice. This verse is where that phrase comes from. If a man is born into this world and born into the spiritual world through Jesus Christ then he only dies once in the flesh. I Corinthians 15:50 **"Now this I say, bretheren, that flesh and blood cannot inherit the kingdom of God; neither doth corruption inherit incorruption."** Baptism is a symbol of this death to the believer in Jesus Christ and being raised from the dead in him with everlasting life. The believer at the moment of his faith is raised from the dead to life everlasting in Jesus Christ. Baptism of a baby does nothing but give a child a bath. It is faith that saves the person and not the baptism. Baptism is a picture of what Christ has done for us in his death on the cross of Calvary. Romans 6:3-6 **"Know ye not, that so many of us as were baptized into Jesus Christ were baptized into his death? Therefore we are buried with him by baptism into death: that like as Christ was raised up from the dead by the glory of the Father, even so we also should walk in newness of life. For id we have been planted together in the likeness of his death, we shall be also in the likeness of his resurrection: Knowing this, that our old man is crucified with him, that the body of sin might be destroyed, that henceforth we should not serve sin."** Those in the second resurrection have only been born one time and must suffer the second death of GEHENNA.

REVELATION CHAPTER 21

John reveals eternity with God the Father and Jesus Christ with the saints. The earth and heaven pass away and the earth is burned up. II Peter 3:10-13 **"But the day of the Lord will come as a thief in the night; in the which the heavens shall pass away with a great noise, and the elements shall melt with fervent heat, the earth also and the works that are therein shall be burned up. Seeing then that all these things shall be dissolved, what manner of persons ought ye to be in all holy conversation and godliness, looking for and hasting unto the coming of the day of God, wherein the heavens being on fire shall be dissolved, and the elements shall melt with fervent heat? Nevertheless we, according to his promise, look for new heavens and a new earth, wherein dwelleth righteousness."** God will create a new heaven and a new earth which will be different from the first earth.

THE CHANGES BETWEEN THE NEW AND THE OLD:

     1.) There will be no sin in the new.

     2.) The new Jerusalem is in heaven and is the center of the universe.

     3.) There will be travel between the new Jerusalem and the new earth.

     4.) There will be no sun.

     5.) Christ will be the light of the new earth.

     6.) There will be no night on the new earth.

     7.) There will be no sea on the new earth.

     8.) God and Jesus Christ will dwell among men.

Vs 1   **"And I saw a new heaven and a new earth: for the first heaven and the first earth were passed away; and there was no more sea."**

Isaiah 65:17 **"For, behold, I create new heavens and a new earth: and the former shall not be remembered, nor come into mind."** The old earth will be destroyed and pass away and will not be remembered any more. This new earth will be beautiful beyond compare to the old earth. There will be many mansions as promised by Jesus. John 14:1-6 **"Let not your heart be troubled: ye believe in God, believe also in me. In my Father's house are many mansions; if it were not so, I would have told you. I go to prepare a place for you. And if I go and prepare a place for you, I will come again, and receive you unto myself; that where I am. there ye may be also. And whither I go ye know, and the way ye know. Thomas saith unto him, Lord we know not whither thou goest; and how can we know the way? Jesus saith unto him, I am the way, the truth, and the life: no man cometh unto the Father, but by me."** The saints will live on the new earth, some will love the mountains, some will love the valleys and everyone will have a mansion. The new earth will not have the curse on the ground for there will be no weeds and thorns anywhere. There will be no sea on the new earth which will increase the land area for the saints to live on. The new earth will be much like it was when God put Adam and Eve in the Garden of Eden.

Vs 2   **"And I John saw the holy city, new Jerusalem, coming down from God out of heaven, prepared as a bride adorned for her husband."**

Jerusalem on the old earth was the center of the earth and the new Jerusalem will be the center of the universe. John is being shown eternity and he saw this himself. This new Jerusalem is where Jesus will dwell with his bride. This will be described later.

Vs 3   **"And I heard a great voice out of heaven saying, Behold, the tabernacle of God is with men, and he will dwell with them, and they shall be his people, and God himself shall be with them, and be their God."**

The new Jerusalem will be the new tabernacle made for all the saints on the earth and for all the bride to dwell with Jesus and with God. There will be travel between the new earth and the new Jerusalem for the saints to come and worship God. There will be no need for a church on the earth, for all will come to the tabernacle in Jerusalem to worship God. Revelation 21:22 **"And I saw no temple therein: for the Lord God Almighty and the Lamb are the temple of it."** This is new for man to have access directly to the throne of God in the new Jerusalem.

Vs 4-5 "And God shall wipe away all tears from their eyes; and there shall be no more death, neither sorrow, nor crying, neither shall there be any more pain: for the former things are passed away. And he that sat upon the throne said, Behold, I make all things new. And he said unto me, Write: for these words are true and faithful."

All rebellion has been put down, all sin and Satan has been defeated and all the results of sin has passed away. There will be no more death, no more sorrow, no more crying, no more pain. All things are made new and the memory of all the former things of this earth will be blotted out of the saints minds. II Corinthians 5:17 "Therefore if any man be in Christ, he is a new creature: old things are passed away; behold, all things are become new." John is commanded to write that all these things that he has seen are just as sure to come to pass as if they already have happened.

Vs 6-8 "And he said unto me, It is done. I am Alpha and Omega, the beginning and the end. I will give unto him that is athirst of the fountain of the water of life freely. He that overcometh shall inherit all things; and I will be his God, and he shall be my son. But the fearful, and unbelieving, and the abominable, and murderers, and whoremongers, and sorcerers, and idolaters, and all liars, shall have their part in the lake which burneth with fire and brimstone: which is the second death."

This new earth and new Jerusalem and all things becoming new will happen just as if it has already happened. It is done. Those who have trusted in Jesus Christ as their Lord and Savior have already inherited all things from the Father and are joint heirs with Jesus Christ right now. Romans 8:17-18 **"And if children, then heirs; heirs of God, and joint-heirs with Christ; if so be that we suffer with him, that we may be also glorified together. For I reckon that the sufferings of this present time are not worthy to be compared with the glory which shall be revealed in us."** The believer in Jesus Christ at the moment he trust in Jesus as his Lord and Savior becomes a joint heir with Christ and shares equally everything that the Father has. Positionally, at the moment of salvation the believer inherits a glorified body just like Christ, he inherits eternal life just like Christ and he inherits the kingdom of God with Christ. All these things are given to the saints not by works that he has done, but the faith he has in God's Son. Ephesians 2:4-9 **But God, who is rich in mercy, for his great love wherewith he loved us, even when we were dead in sins, hath quickened us together with Christ, (by grace are ye saved) and hath raised us up together, and made us sit together in heavenly places in Christ Jesus: That in the ages to come he might show the exceeding riches of his grace in his kindness toward us through Christ Jesus. <u>For by grace are ye saved through faith; and that not of yourselves; it is a gift of God: Not of works, least any man should boast.</u>"** Man will serve either Father God or father Satan. Man will inherit eternal life from Father God or he will inherit eternal damnation from father Satan. Man makes the choice of whose child he will be by whom he serves. I John 5:4-5 **"For whatsoever is born of God overcometh the world: and this is the victory that overcometh the world, even our faith. Who is he that overcometh the world, but he that believeth that Jesus is the Son of God."** I John 3:2 **"Beloved, now are we the sons of God, and it doth not yet appear what we shall be: but we know that, when he shall appear, we shall be like him; for we shall see him as he is."**

WHO ARE GOING TO HADES:

1.) The fearful- those who are afraid to die and have no hope.

2.) The unbelieving- all the unbelieving go to hell.

3.) The abominable- vile, nasty, disgusting and disagreeable persons.

4.) Murderers- all murder comes from Satan who is the father of murder.

5.) Whoremongers- women chasers that live for sexual desires.

6.) Sorcerers- these are the drug users and the seller of drugs.

7.) idolaters- those that put anything before God and his Son Jesus Christ.

8.) All liars- habitual liars that do not even know the truth.

Vs 9-10 **"And there came unto me one of the seven angels which had the seven vials full of the seven last plagues, and talked with me, saying, Come hither, I will show thee the bride, the Lambs wife. And he carried me away in the spirit to**

a great and high mountain, and showed me that great city, the holy

Jerusalem, descending out of heaven from God."

This angel is similar to the angel in chapter seventeen that shows John the

destruction of the two Babylons and explains what John was seeing. This may be

the same angel that is now showing John the new Jerusalem coming down from

God out of heaven. John is being given a guided tour through the future events

that must shortly come to pass. John is carried to high mountain where he is

shown the new Jerusalem coming down like a new moon from heaven. There

may not be a moon around the earth because it is not mentioned here. The new

Jerusalem may be a heavenly body like the old moon that we know today. We are

told by John that there will be no night and that the new Jerusalem will be the

light of the new earth. There may not be a need for a moon to give light by

night.!

Vs 11-14 **"Having the glory of God: and her light was like unto a stone most**

precious, even like a jasper stone, clear as crystal; And had a wall great and

high, and had twelve gates, and at the gates twelve angels, and names written

thereon, which are the names of the twelve tribes of the children of Israel:

On the east three gates; on the north three gates; on the south three gates; on

the west three gates. And the wall of the city had twelve foundations, and in

them the names of the twelve apostles of the Lamb."

The picture of the new Jerusalem that John paints with the words of a first
century man is hard to understand. The new Jerusalem is a heavenly body
coming down out of heaven and it looks like a diamond or a jasper stone. The
new Jerusalem is pictured with twelve foundations of precious stones with light
radiating out from the center of the stone. New Jerusalem is like a twelve sided
soccer ball with each side being a different colored precious stone. Revelation
21:23-24 **"And the city had no need of the sun, neither the moon, to shine in
it; for the glory of God did lighten it, and the Lamb is the light thereof. And
the nations of them which are saved shall walk in the light of it."** The picture
is of Jesus at the center of the new Jerusalem as the light of it and the light of the
earth. The light of Jesus radiates through each foundation of all the colors of the
rainbow and is like a sparkling diamond in the sky. "The wall of the city" is
singular as one wall and it has twelve foundations. The wall and the foundations
are one and the same. In this twelve sided diamond in the sky there were three
gates in each of the four directions of the compass. Each of the twelve gates were
of a single pearl. The gates are round and fit into the twelve foundations of the
spherical shaped city. The foundations are the outside wall of the city and the
saints enter through the pearly gates to the inside of the new Jerusalem and walk
around the inside of the foundations. With Jesus as the light of the world and the
center of the new Jerusalem and the light radiating through the twelve
foundations of precious stones will look like a rainbow of light being cast onto

the new earth. Revelation 4:3 **"And he that sat was to look upon like a jasper and a sardine stone: and there was a rainbow round about the throne, in sight like unto an emerald."**

The foundations were named after the twelve apostles. Jesus is the corner stone and the twelve apostles are the foundations on which the gospel message went out into all the earth and was what the church was built on. The new Jerusalem is for the bride of Christ to live in with her husband and will be predominantly the gentiles that were saved during the church age. It is fitting that the foundations are named after the twelve apostles.

Vs 15-17 **"And he that talked with me had a golden reed to measure the city, and the gates thereof, and the wall thereof. And the city lieth foursquare, and the length is as large as the breadth: and he measured the city with the reed, twelve thousand furlongs. The length and the breadth and the height of it are equal. And he measured the wall thereof, a hundred and forty and four cubits, according to the measure of a man, that is, of the angel."**

A cubit is the measurement from the tip of the middle finger to the end of the elbow which is about one and one half feet. The furlong is about six hundred and sixty feet or about one eight of a mile. The angel measures the new Jerusalem for John and it is his measurement that John corrects himself in using the angels cubit measurement. The thickness of the wall or the foundation that encircles the new city of Jerusalem is one hundred forty-four cubits or about one hundred twenty six feet. The height, width and the breadth are all equal to twelve thousand furlongs or about fifteen hundred miles. This is almost the size of the moon in comparison. Some Bible scholars believe the new Jerusalem to be a cube with twelve levels of foundations. It would be hard to explain how in a cube that the river of life could flow around through all twelve foundations and how everyone could have equal access to Jesus at the center of it. If you picture the river of life flowing around the inside face of a sphere and the tree of life growing on both sides of the river, then the river is continuous with no end. All the inhabitants have equal access to Jesus at the center of the sphere.

Vs 18-20 **"And the building of the wall of it was of jasper: and the city was pure gold, like unto clear glass. And the foundations of the wall of the city were garnished with all manner of precious stones. The first foundation was jasper; the second, sapphire; the third, chalcedony; the fourth, an emerald; the fifth, sardonyx; the sixth, sardis; the seventh, chrysolite; the eighth, beryl; the ninth, a topaz; the tenth, a chrysoprasus; the eleventh, a jacinth; the twelfth, an amethyst."**

I understand that if gold was refined to a pure state, that it would be clear as glass. This is the picture John paints for us here in this verse. The streets are pure gold as crystal glass. The foundations of the wall of the city are twelve precious stones. The wall and the foundations are the same. Notice that the foundations are all colors of the rainbow in these precious stones.

Vs 21 **"And the twelve gates were twelve pearls; every several gate was of one pearl; and the street of the city is pure gold, as it were transparent glass."**

The pearly gates of heaven or more accurately the pearly gates of the new Jerusalem are open for all on the earth to come into to worship the Lord Jesus Christ at all times. The streets are pure gold and all that stand there will have equal access to the one who is the light of this world at the center of the new Jerusalem.

Vs 22 **'And I saw no temple therein: for the Lord God Almighty and the Lamb are the temple of it."**

When John opened the Revelation he saw a temple in the first heaven and the ark of the covenant. Jesus was pictured as our high priest who ministered at the throne of God in our behalf. This is the picture of heaven today as Paul records in Hebrews chapter five through chapter ten. Man no longer needs a high priest on the earth to take his petitions and sacrifices into the holy of holies as they did before Jesus Christ's resurrection. Today, Jesus is our high priest where we can go through him directly to the throne of God without a man's intercession. We pray directly to Jesus Christ and our prayers are heard at all times of the day and night. Hebrews 10:11-14 **"And every priest standeth daily ministering and offering oftentimes the same sacrifices, which can never take away sins: But this man, after he had offered one sacrifice for sins for ever, sat down on the right hand of God. From henceforth expecting till his enemies be made his footstool. For by one offering he hath perfected for ever them that are sanctified."** Romans 8:34 **"It is Christ that died, yea rather, that is risen again, who is even at the right hand of God, who also maketh intercession for us."** In the new Jerusalem there will not be a temple or a holy of holies, for all men will have access to the throne of God as high priest themselves. Revelation 1:6 **"And hath made us kings and priest unto God and his Father; to him be glory and dominion for ever and ever. Amen."** The saved are made kings and priest in the new Jerusalem and the new earth.

Vs 23-25 **"And the city had no need of the sun, neither of the moon, to shine in it: for the glory of God did lighten it, and the Lamb is the light thereof. And the nations of them which are saved shall walk in the light of it: and the kings of the earth do bring their glory and honor of the nations into it. And the gates of it shall not be shut at all by day: for there shall be no night there. And they shall bring the glory and honor of the nations into it."**

John 8:12 **"Then spake Jesus again unto them, saying, I am the light of the world: he that followeth me shall not walk in darkness, but shall have the light of life."** Jesus is the light of the new Jerusalem and the light of the new earth. Jesus light will never go out, so there will be no night. The saved are made kings and priest and the kings on the earth will come to the new Jerusalem to bring their worship to Jesus Christ and to God the Father. All the earth will worship in the new Jerusalem. There will be travel back and forth between the two. With a glorified body like Jesus, the saved will be able to live without air and without food. They will have access to the fountain of living water and the fruit of the tree of life in the new Jerusalem.

Vs 27 **"And there shall in no wise enter into it any thing that defileth, neither whatsoever worketh abomination, or maketh a lie: but they which are written in the Lamb's book of life."**

This verse excludes all flesh in the natural body and there will be no more flesh, only those who have a resurrected body like that of Jesus who are written in the Lamb's book of life. All flesh has been destroyed and only those who have trusted in Jesus as their Lord and Savior are on the new earth and in the new Jerusalem.

REVELATION CHAPTER 22

John continues from chapter twenty-one with one of the seven angels which had the seven bowls full of the seven last plagues explaining to him the things he saw and is given a guided tour of the new Jerusalem and the new earth. This chapter brings us to the close of the Bible with the final scene in eternity and the final words of God and his Son Jesus Christ. Genesis opens with God dwelling with man on this earth and Revelation closes with God dwelling with man in heaven for eternity.

Vs 1-2 **"And he showed me a pure river of water of life, clear as crystal, proceeding out of the throne of God and of the Lamb. In the midst of the street of it, and on either side of the river, was there the tree of life, which bare twelve manner of fruits, and yielded her fruit every month: and the leaves of the tree were for healing of the nations."**

There will be a river of the water of life flowing through the new Jerusalem from the throne of God and the Lamb. When God created the garden of Eden for Adam to live in, he did not put the river of life on the earth. God planted the tree of life and the tree of knowledge and evil in the middle of the garden. There have been men that have searched the world over for the fountain of life that they could live forever and remain young. There is no fountain of youth on the earth, but there was at one time a tree of life that gave eternal life to those who ate of it. It would seem that this tree may still exist on the earth, but even if it did, God placed a guard around the tree of life to keep man from gaining

access to it. Not until this time in the new Jerusalem is it offered to all the saints

that go there. Genesis 2:8-9 **"And the Lord God planted a garden eastward in**

Eden; and there he put the man whom he had formed. And out of the ground

made the Lord God to grow every tree that is pleasant to the sight, and good

for food; the tree of life also in the midst of the garden, and the tree of

knowledge and evil." After Adam and Eve sinned by eating of the forbidden

fruit of tree of knowledge and evil, God closed the garden of Eden to man.

Genesis 3:24 **"So he drove out the man; and he placed at the east of the**

garden of Eden cherubim, and a flaming sword which turned every way, to

keep the way of the tree of life." The only way man has access to the tree of life

is by faith in Jesus Christ as his Lord and Savior and entering eternity in the new

Jerusalem. Nothing is said about the tree of knowledge and evil being blocked

from man. The tree of life may have been moved when the flood came in Noah's

days, if not it is still guarded today and man cannot get to it. The curse of the

flesh was to die and not to dwell in the presence of God. From that day Adam

sinned, he began to die in the flesh. Actually what God told Adam is that in

dying you shall surly die. Without forgiveness of his sins Adam would surly die

eternally as well as dying physically. God pointed out the way for forgiveness

through the shed blood of the sacrifice of the Lamb of God. Animals were killed

and sacrificed and their skins were their first clothing. The old testament saints

were saved the same way we are saved today. They were looking forward to the coming of the Lamb of God and we today are looking back to when the Lamb of God came to die on the cross. Only through the shed blood of Jesus Christ can a man have eternal life. By eating of the tree of life in the new Jerusalem the saints will live for eternity. The tree of life yields twelve kinds of fruit, every month. There are twelve months and a different kind of fruit in every month.

Vs 3-4 **"And there shall be no more curse: but the throne of God and of the Lamb shall be in it; and his servants shall serve him: And they shall see his face; and his name shall be in their foreheads."**

Genesis 3:17-19 **"And unto Adam he said, Because thou hast harkened unto the voice of thy wife, and hast eaten of the tree, of which I commanded thee, saying, Thou shalt not eat of it: cursed is the ground for thy sake; in sorrow shall thou eat of it all the days of thy life; thorns also and thistles shall it bring forth to thee; and thou shalt eat the herb of the field: In the sweat of thy face shalt thou eat bread, till thou return unto the ground; for out of it wast thou taken: for dust thou art, and unto dust thou shalt return."** The curse on the ground will be removed in the new earth to like it was in the garden of Eden. God and the Lamb will again live with man and will see his face. No man in the flesh can look upon the face of Almighty God who is holy and righteous. Moses was allowed to see the shadow of God as he passed by, but could not look upon his face. In the new Jerusalem the saved will see his face and wear his name in their foreheads.

Vs 5 **"And there shall be no night there; and they need no candle, neither light of the sun; for the Lord God giveth them light: and they shall reign for ever and ever."**

There will be no need of oil to generate electricity, nor automobiles, nor airplanes, nor to heat homes and light homes. Everything will beautiful and natural. The saved will travel like the Lord Jesus Christ and have power to do all things in the new Jerusalem and the new earth. All the things that Jesus did while he was on this earth, the saints will be able to do in the new earth and the new Jerusalem. Some may say they will miss the sun and the moon and nighttime, but there is no comparison to what we know today to what it will be like in the new earth and the new Jerusalem.

Vs 6-7 **"And he said unto me, These sayings are faithful and true: and the Lord God of the holy prophets sent his angel to show unto his servants the things which must shortly be done. Behold, I come quickly: blessed is he that keepeth the sayings of the prophesy of this book."**

This angel tells John that these things that he is writing are faithful and true and that John has been sent to show these things to the servants of Jesus Christ. These things that John has written are shortly coming to pass. Jesus is coming for his bride soon and when he comes it will be quickly. I Corinthians 15:52 **"In a moment, in the twinkling of an eye, at the last trump: for the trumpet shall sound, and the dead shall be raised incorruptible, and we shall be changed."** When Jesus Comes for his bride no one will see it happen, the bride will be taken and be gone. Blessed are those who believe in the Jesus Christ and are part of the rapture of the bride. Blessed are those who look forward to the coming of the Son of God and those who read the Revelation given to John. Three times in this chapter this angel tells John "Behold, I come quickly."

Vs 8-10 **"And I John saw these things, and heard them. And when I had heard and seen, I fell down to worship before the feet of the angel which showed me these things. Then saith he unto me, See thou do it not: for I am thy fellow servant, and of thy brethren the prophets, and of them which keep the sayings of this book: worship God. And he saith unto me, Seal not the sayings of the prophesy of this book: for the time is at hand."**

For those who say that John was dreaming all of what he wrote in Revelation must have missed this verse. Revelation 22:19 **"And if any man shall take away from the words of the book of this prophesy, God shall take**

away his part out of the book of life, and out of the holy city, and from the things which are written in this book." Those who choose not to believe the prophesy of the book of Revelation and choose to reject the creation account in Genesis might as well worship Satan for as much good it will do them when they stand before Jesus Christ to give account of their unbelief. It has been said "the Bible says it, I believe it and that settles it." It does not matter about the middle part and could be said "the Bible says it and that settles it." John is overcome with worship of God for what he has seen and falls at the feet of this angel speaking with him and worships him. The words of this angel seem to baffle us when he is called an angel and also is a fellow servant, a Jew and a prophet. This angel is also one of the seven angels that have the seven bowls of the final judgments of God on the earth. The simple explanation would be that this angel is Jesus Christ and he identifies himself as the one who says **"Behold, I come quickly"** three times in this chapter. John is commanded to worship God for at the moment he is pictured as an angel performing as a servant of God himself. This was the picture given to us when Jesus was on this earth as a servant of God, doing his will in giving of himself as the Lamb to be slain for the sins of the world. John is commanded to not to seal up the prophesy of this book but is for the saints to read to reveal what must shortly come to pass.

Vs 11 "He that is unjust, let him be unjust still: and he which is filthy, let him be

filthy still: and he that is righteous, let him be righteous still: and he that is

holy, let him be holy still."

The unjust and filthy man will reject the word of God and choose not to

believe the Word of God and he will remain unjust and filthy through eternity.

The righteous and holy man will accept the word of God and will remain

righteous and holy through eternity. Only the righteous and holy man that has the

blood of Jesus to forgive them of their sins will have access to the tree of life in

the new Jerusalem in eternity. All those that reject the words of this book of

Revelation and the Word of God will remain filthy and unjust or unjustified in the

sight of God.

Vs 12 "And, behold, I come quickly; and my reward is with me, to give every man

according as his work shall be."

This is a promise to those that look for his coming and that his rewards for

the works of them that believe in him are with him. I Thessalonians 4:13-18

"But I would not have you to be ignorant, brethren, concerning them which

are asleep, that ye sorrow not, even as others which have no hope. For if we

believe that Jesus died and rose again, even so them also which sleep in Jesus

will God bring with him. For this we say unto you by the word of the Lord,

that we which are alive and remain unto the coming of the Lord shall not prevent them which are asleep. For the Lord himself shall descend from heaven with a shout, with the trump of God: and the dead in Christ shall rise first: Then we which are alive and remain shall be caught up together with them in the clouds, to meet the Lord in the air: and so shall we ever be with the Lord. Wherefore comfort one another with these words." The next great event in God's timetable is the rapture of the saints, or the church or the bride of Christ. The bride looks for her husband to come for her and is anxious to see him. Those that are already dead and have trusted in Jesus as their Lord and Savior will rise up first and then those that are still alive will be caught up together with the dead to meet Jesus in the air. Matthew 6:19-21 **"Lay not up for yourselves treasures upon earth, where moth and rust doth corrupt, and where thieves break through and steel: But lay up for yourselves treasures in heaven, where neither moth nor rust doth corrupt, and where thieves do not break through nor steal: For where your treasure is, there will your heart be also."** Matthew 16:27 **"For the Son of man shall come in the glory of his Father with the angels; and then shall he reward every man according to his works."** I Corinthians 3:12-15 **"Now if any man build upon this foundation gold, silver, precious stones, wood, hay, stubble; Every man's work shall be made manifest: for the day shall declare it, because it shall be revealed by fire; and the fire shall try every man's work of what sort it is. If any man's work abide which he hath built thereupon, he shall receive a reward. If any**

man's work shall be burned, he shall suffer loss: but he himself shall be saved; yet so as by fire." There will be many in the rapture that will have works that abide and works that he will suffer loss from and the net result will be that he stands there before Jesus empty handed. There are gold, silver and precious stones rewards and there are wood, hay and stubble rewards. When the eyes of Jesus look upon our rewards they are tested with fire. The gold, silver and precious stones are made pure with fire and the wood, hay and stubble are burned up with fire. Our rewards will be revealed for what kind they are.

Vs 13-15 **"I am Alpha and Omega, the beginning and the end, the first and the last. Blessed are they that do his commandments, that they may have right to the tree of life, and may enter in through the gates onto the city. For without are dogs, and sorcerers, and whoremongers, and murderers, and idolaters, and whosoever loveth and maketh a lie."**

The angel that is speaking to John is now identified as the Son of God himself. Jesus affirms his deity with God the Father as the beginning and the end. This is how Jesus identified himself when he first appeared to Jon on the Isle of Patmos. Revelation 1:11 **"Saying, I am Alpha and Omega, the first and the last: and what thou seest, write in a book, and send it unto the seven churches which are in Asia."** Another blessing is placed on all who keep the commandments of Jesus that they may enter the new Jerusalem and have access to the tree of life. The commandments of Jesus were given before in that we are to love the Lord our God with all our heart, mind and soul; and that we are to love our brother as we love ourselves. Those that do not keep his commandments then are dogs, sorcerers, whoremongers, murderers, idolators and all liars.

Vs 16-17 **"I Jesus have sent mine angel to testify unto you these things in the churches. I am the root and the offspring of David, and the bright and morning star. And the Spirit and the bride say, Come. And let him that heareth say, Come. And let him that is athirst come. And whosoever will, let him take the water of life freely."**

John is called an angel which in the explanation of chapter one verse twenty refers to the pastors of the seven churches. John bears witness of all the things written in this book of Revelation and that Jesus is the promised seed of David and the bright and morning star that rose from the grave. John has seen all these things first hand and bears witness that they are true. The universal invitation goes out to whosoever will, let him come unto Jesus and drink of the river of living water. John 4:13-14 **"Jesus answered and said unto her, Whosoever drinketh of this water shall thirst again: But whosoever drinketh of the water that I shall give him shall never thirst; but the water that I shall give him shall be in him a well of water springing up into everlasting life."** The Samaritan woman desired the water Jesus offered her and all that desire this water are welcome to come unto Jesus and he will give it to them freely. The

Holy Spirit and the bride or the church are being used today to call out of the

world those who will come unto the Lord Jesus Christ. This is the job of the

church and the Holy Spirit today.

Vs 18-19 **"For I testify unto every man that heareth the words of the prophesy of**

this book, If any man shall add unto these things, God shall add unto him the

plagues that are written in this book: And if any man shall take away from

the words of the book of this prophesy, God shall take away his part out of

the book of life, and out of the holy city, and from the things which are

written in this book."

We see the final invitation and the final warning of Jesus in the Bible. Let

whosoever come that will come unto Jesus. Let whosoever that denies the

prophesy of this book be cast into everlasting torment into GEHENNA for their

name will not be in the book of life. I Corinthians 2:12-16 **"Now we have**

received, not the spirit of the world, but the spirit which is of God; that we

might know the things that are freely given to us of God. Which things also

we speak, not in the words which man's wisdom teacheth, but which the Holy

Ghost teacheth; comparing spiritual things with spiritual. But the natural

man receiveth not the things of the Spirit of God; for they are foolishness

unto him: neither can he know them, because they are spiritually discerned.

But he that is spiritual judgeth all things, yet he himself is judged of no man. For who hath known the mind of the Lord, that he may instruct him? But we have the mind of Christ." The lost man will think everything in the book of Revelation is foolishness and does not understand them because they are spiritual and the Holy Spirit will reveal these things to our understanding. Can a man go to heaven who says that this book is not the word of God? Jesus tells us that if a man takes away from the book of Revelation then he will take his name out of the book of life.

Vs 20-21 **"He which testifieth these things saith, Surely I come quickly. Amen. Even so, come, Lord Jesus. The grace of our Lord Jesus Christ be with you all. Amen."**

We have the promise of Jesus that he is coming back for us and he is coming soon. There will be no time for someone to see his coming and fall on his knees to ask forgiveness for there will not be enough time. His coming is the twinkling of the eye and it is over. Man has to make a decision to follow Jesus or to follow Satan. He is a servant of one or the other. A man can not serve two masters for he will love one and hate the other. All Christians should be like John in saying **"Even so, come, Lord Jesus."**